TWENTY-FOUR CONVERSATIONS

WITH BORGES

Including a Selection of Poems

Illustration by Roberto Páez

TWENTY-FOUR CONVERSATIONS

WITH BORGES

Including a Selection of Poems

INTERVIEWS BY ROBERTO ALIFANO 1981-1983

Conversations translated by Nicomedes Suárez Araúz,
Willis Barnstone and Noemí Escandell

Poems translated by Willis Barnstone, Jorge Luis Borges
and Nicomedes Suárez Araúz

Photographs by Willis Barnstone

Altamira Inter-American Series
LASCAUX PUBLISHERS

An Altamira Inter-American Edition

Published by Lascaux Publishers
        P.O. Box 564
        Housatonic, MA 01236

Library of Congress Catalog Card Number: 83-082930

ISBN: 0-394-62192-1

Distributed by Grove Press, Inc.
196 West Houston Street
New York, N.Y. 10014

Copy editor: Ruth Melnick

Manufactured in the United States of America
   by Excelsior Printing Company
        North Adams, Massachusetts

In Memory of Archibald MacLeish

"When I was a child in the eighteen nineties there was a sense in the United States of a common American cause which found expression of sorts in the war for the liberation of Cuba. That sense was founded on a knowledge of the lives of the great liberators, both Latin and Anglo-Saxon, of that century, and the common experience of all the American peoples. But it was a feeble sense at best. And yet there is, I think, something the writers—particularly the young writers—can do: A common effort to recompose, restore, a conception, not of a country, a group of countries, but a vast continent stretched from north to south across the turning of the earth—the human journey. If there could be a journal or a press dedicated to the three great languages of the Americas, to bring to life the common experience of our peoples, to restore to vitality their common hopes, it might silence those out-dated politicians who have come to power in my country, in so many of our countries. We might sail with Columbus again and see the flowering branches on the water."

From a conversation with the Bolivian poet
Nicomedes Suárez Araúz
June 6, July 12, 1981

Archibald MacLeish inspired and supported the founding of Altamira/Lascaux.

Contents

DEDICATION *v*
WORKS BY BORGES *ix*
ACKNOWLEDGMENTS *xi*
PROLOGUE BY ROBERTO ALIFANO *xiii*

1. Some Personal Memories *1*
2. Facing the Year 1983 *11*
3. Memories of a Trip to Japan *17*
4. The Labyrinth and the Tiger *23*
5. Funes and Insomnia *27*
6. Books *31*
7. Poetry *37*
8. The Detective Story *43*
9. Translation *49*
10. North American Literature *55*
11. Time *61*
12. The Kabbalah *65*
13. The Tango *69*
14. Arturo Capdevilla *75*
15. Evaristo Carriego *83*
16. Cervantes *89*
17. Dante *93*
18. Ricardo Güiraldes *99*
19. Nathaniel Hawthorne *103*
20. Rudyard Kipling *107*
21. Quevedo and Lugones *111*
22. Xul Solar *117*
23. Virgil *121*
24. Oscar Wilde *125*

A SELECTION OF POEMS BY BORGES *131*

The Other Tiger *133*

Poem Written in a Copy of Beowulf *134*

In Praise of Shadow *135*

The Unending Rose *137*

That Nothing is Known *138*

A Blind Man *138*

I Am *139*

The Blind Man I *139*

The Blind Man II *140*

On His Blindness *140*

The White Deer *141*

Ephialtes *141*

The Conquistador *142*

The Suicide *142*

My Books *143*

The Panther *143*

Browning Resolves to be a Poet *144*

Brunanburh, 937 A.D. *145*

Dream *145*

The Nightingale *146*

Heraclitus *147*

A Key in East Lansing *148*

Remorse *148*

Nightmare *149*

Ein Traum *149*

Johannes Brahms *150*

G.L. Bürger *151*

The Causes *152*

Endymion on Latmos *153*

A Saturday *154*

The Moon *154*

Music Box *155*

1982 *157*

Possession of Yesterday *158*

WORKS BY BORGES

Fervor de Buenos Aires, 1923
Inquisiciones, 1925
Luna de enfrente, 1925
Cuaderno San Martín, 1929
Evaristo Carriego, 1930
Discusión, 1932
Historia universal de la infamia

1935

Historia de la eternidad

1936

Ficciones, 1944
El aleph, 1949
Otras inquisiciones, 1952
El hacedor, 1960
El otro, el mismo, 1964
Para las seis cuerdas, 1965
Elogio de la sombra, 1969
El informe de Brodie, 1970
El oro de los tigres, 1972
Obras completas, 1974
La rosa profunda, 1975
Libro de arena, 1975
La moneda de hierro, 1976
Historia de la noche, 1977

IN COLLABORATION WITH ADOLFO BIOY CASARES

Seis problemas para don Isidro Parodi, 1942
Un modelo para la muerte, 1946
Dos fantasías memorables, 1946
Crónicas de Bustos Domecq, 1967

IN ENGLISH TRANSLATION

Ficciones, 1962
Labyrinths, 1962
Other Inquisitions, 1962
Dreamtigers, 1964
A Personal Anthology, 1967
The Book of Imaginary Beings, 1969
The Aleph and Other Stories, 1933-1969

   1970

Doctor Brodie's Report, 1971
A Universal History of Infamy, 1972
Selected Poems, 1923-1967

   1972

In Praise of Darkness, 1974
Chronicles of Bustos Domecq, 1976
The Book of Sand, 1977
The Gold of the Tigers, 1977
Six Problems for Don Isidro Parodi, 1981

ACKNOWLEDGMENTS

Some of the interviews presented in this book have previously appeared in magazines. Chapter 11, "Time," was published in *Nightsun*, no. 2, 1982, copyright © 1982 by *Nightsun*; chapter 7, "Poetry," was published in *American Poetry Review*, 12, no. 6, 1983, copyright © 1983 by *American Poetry Review*; chapters 1 and 4, "Some Personal Memories" and "The Labyrinth and the Tiger," respectively, appeared in *The Massachusetts Review*, winter, 1984, copyright © 1984 by The Massachusetts Review, Inc.

For permission to reprint Willis Barnstone's translations of poems by Jorge Luis Borges, Lascaux Publishers is indebted to: Bantam Books, Inc., for "Poem Written in a Copy of Beowulf," "Heraclitus," "A Key in East Lansing" and "Remorse," from *Modern European Poetry*, ed. by Willis Barnstone, copyright © 1966, 1977 by Bantam Books, Inc.; *Chicago Review* for "The Other Tiger" and "The Conquistador," from *Chicago Review* 27, no. 4, and "Ein Traum" from *Chicago Review*, 28, no. 3, copyright © 1976 and 1977 by *Chicago Review*; *Holiday Magazine* for "The Unending Rose," "That Nothing is Known," "A Blind Man," "The White Deer," and "The Suicide," from *Holiday Magazine*, January-February, 1976; "Nightmare," from *Holiday Magazine*, March, 1976, copyright © 1976 by *Holiday Magazine; "Brunanburh, 937 A.D." from American Poetry Review*, 5, copyright © 1976 by *American Poetry Review*; Indiana University Press, for "G.L. Bürger," "The Causes," "Endymion at Latmos" and "The Moon," from *Borges at Eighty; Conversations*, ed. by Willis Barnstone, copyright © 1982 by Indiana University Press; University of Press at Orono Press for "A Saturday" and "Music Box," from *Simply a Man of Letters*, ed. by Carlos Cortínez, copyright © 1982 by University of Maine at Orono Press; Holmes and Meir Company for "In Praise of Shadow" (tr. by Anthony and Willis Barnstone), from *The Poetics of Ecstasy* by Willis Barnstone, copyright © 1983 by Holmes and Meir.

Lascaux Publishers is grateful to E.P. Dutton & Co., Inc. for permission to publish Willis Barnstone's translations "Browning Resolves To Be a Poet," "I Am," "The Blind Man I," "The Blind Man II," "The Nightingale," "My Books" and "Dream." These poems were previously translated by Alastair Reid and were included in the book, *The Gold of The Tigers*, copyright © 1977 by E.P. Dutton.

Dr. Nicomedes Suárez Araúz, Director of Intercultural Studies for Latin America at Simon's Rock of Bard College, and Dr. Willis Barnstone, Professor of Comparative Literature at Indiana University, translated most of the interviews presented here. Others were done by Dr. Suárez Araúz and Dr. Noemí Escandell, Professor of Spanish at Westfield State College.

Lascaux Publishers is grateful to Ruth Melnick for acting as our copy editor. We are thankful to Dr. Robert Ackerman and Dr. John Paskus of Simon's Rock of Bard College for proofreading and revising the final version of the translation of the interviews.

Prologue

A special closeness to friends makes the task of writing about them very difficult. In writing about Jorge Luis Borges, I find myself in such a quandary. I am most fortunate to be his friend, to have shared many intimate moments, to have collaborated with him on various projects.

Borges has said that his life has lacked life and death, but my perception of him is contrary to his opinion of himself. As a man and literary figure, Borges, I find, does indeed live fully. His manner of living, needless to say, is unique. It is well known that Borges loves to lose himself in the serene pleasures of reason, reverie and imagination, which are the foundations of his literary world. He also enjoys envisioning himself as a character in his marvelous literary universe. Nevertheless, he is a man who glories in the simple things of the earth and of human existence. His life consists of an odd mixture of abstract literary and philosophical preoccupations and the myriad aspects of his personal existence: bread and the hourglass, friendship and Spinoza, time and the fragrance of a thistle, tea at five and Stevenson, rice and the exacting rigor of metrics, the *milonga* and Gibbon's *Decline and Fall of the Roman Empire*, silence and metaphor, the caress of the sun on his face and Carriego's poetry, *dulce de leche*[1] and *Don Quixote*, his military ancestors and the wit of Oscar Wilde, the fall of leaves in autumn and Kipling's prose, beautiful women and labyrinths, libraries and Whitman's poetry, the harsh taste of misfortune and Buddhism.

I first met Borges when he was a gallant young man of more than sixty years. I was then little more than a child; I am considerably older now, but he has turned eighty-four, and though he has tried his utmost to age, he has not been able to. He is the same vital man I used to wait for at the entrance to the National Library to discuss or to attack his favorite themes. He still retains the battling spirit of his youth. He does not turn away from any

---

[1]A typical Argentine jam made from milk, sugar and cinnamon.

hardship—constant and exacting literary creation, exhausting trips to other countries, or lecture tours. He does it all with the same enthusiasm of his earlier years. He has the same delight in exchanging jokes with strangers and with friends, the same delight in interesting conversations and debates. The Borges I know is a resourceful and fearful polemist; one could fittingly apply to him an observation someone made about Doctor Johnson that if his pistol erred, he would hold it by the barrel and beat one with its handle.

Whether in conversations or in his literary work, Borges is a master of dialogue. Bernard Shaw defined a dialogue as an infinite process that renders the intangible tangible and the impossible possible. In a dialogue, the thoughts and dreams of the speaker establish a correspondence to those of the listener. The oral and written work of Borges has that essential quality; it is a triumph of communication between human beings. There may be differences between Borges's oral and written voices, but they both share the same imaginative ideas—profound and beautiful in their expression. Borges always startles with the spontaneous yet elegant phrase; clichés are foreign to his speech.

The conversations presented here began four years ago at the suggestion of an international newspaper chain. Initially, the paper proposed that Borges write a weekly article for distribution in several languages. He answered that his blindness and the lack of a secretary would prevent him from doing so. He suggested that, instead, those articles take the form of dialogues, that is, by holding conversations with a questioner who would then be in charge of transcribing them. This alternative was accepted, and Borges suggested that I be the questioner. Regrettably, soon after we started the assignment, the paper had to discontinue all its projects in Argentina, and the work was left dangling. Nevertheless, my interest in the dialogues continued, and we carried out many others. Borges spoke about almost everything: he reviewed his literary themes, his personal concerns, his life and the life of others. Our method of conducting these dialogues was simple. With the tape recorder on, I would initiate a subject. Borges willingly and eloquently would answer. He never set any restrictions. And so, more than forty cassette tapes recorded his memories and thoughts about a multiplicity of topics.

Some months ago, Altamira/Lascaux Publishers, an Inter-American Press in the United States, suggested the possibility of compiling and publishing these conversations. As a result these pieces found their way way into another language.

This work is essentially the creation of Jorge Luis Borges; it is part of his marvelous universe. My participation in it is minimal. This work is yet another gift from a great master, to whom I am especially indebted and to whom his readers owe so much. This is the gift of a man who measures the world with long steps, often stopping to laugh, to love, to contemplate and to astound.

Roberto Alifano
Buenos Aires
August 1983

1

Some Personal Memories

> I met the *guapo*, Nicolás Paredes, ...
> He lived in abject poverty, and before I
> left, he said: "No one leaves my house
> empty-handed, Borges." And as he
> couldn't find anything else to give me,
> he gave me an orange, which I would
> have liked to preserve forever.

ROBERTO ALIFANO: Borges, I suggest that we talk specifically about you. Can we evoke, for example, your first readings as a child, your first acquaintance with literature, your parents, your sister Norah, your friends, your teachers?

JORGE LUIS BORGES: Yes, why not—I am open to any question.

ALIFANO: What was your first literary reading, Borges?

BORGES: I believe that my first reading was Grimms' *Fairy Tales* in an English version. I was very young, I don't know exactly how young, but I can't remember a time in my childhood when I didn't know how to read or write. I was educated by my father's library, perhaps more than by high school or the university. Much of that formation I owe to my grandmother, who was English and knew the Bible by heart. So I could say that I came upon literature via the Holy Ghost and by the verses I used to hear at home. My mother, for example, knew by heart *El Fausto* by Estanislao del Campo.

ALIFANO: Your education was also bilingual, wasn't it?

BORGES: Yes, at home my English grandmother spoke her native language; the rest of the family spoke Spanish. I was very young but knew that with my maternal grandmother, Leonor Acevedo de Suárez, I had to speak Spanish, and that with my paternal grandmother, Frances Haslam Arnett, I had to speak English. As for my readings, those I remember were first in English, since my father's library had mainly English books. Also, around that time, I read some books together with my sister Norah. I believe they

1

were stories by Poe and novels by Hugo, Dumas and Walter Scott.

ALIFANO: Did you share a lot of things with your sister Norah during your childhood?

BORGES: Yes, I am only two years older than she is, and naturally our childhoods merged. Norah was always the one who came up with ideas for games. I was shy and always remained in the background. She later devoted herself to painting. Norah is a great painter. When we were children and we moved to Adrogué, her interest in painting began. And in Switzerland, guided by a tutor, she perfected her art.

ALIFANO: Did you finish high school in Switzerland?

BORGES: Yes. And that was fortunate for me, for I was a good student of Latin, and I wrote verse in Latin with the help of the *Gradus ad Parnassum* by Guicherat. My favorite readings in Latin were Seneca and Tacitus.

ALIFANO: What year did your family move to Switzerland, Borges?

BORGES: In 1914. We lived there throughout the First World War. I remember that in one week I saw the mobilization of about three hundred thousand men to defend the border. The Swiss armed forces had only three colonels, and it was proposed that one of them be promoted to the rank of general for the duration of the war. Colonel Odéou, who was our neighbor, was chosen for the post; and he accepted on the condition that his salary not be increased. How odd, isn't it? In Argentina the complete opposite happens: there are more generals than tanks and more admirals than ships, and they spend their lives giving themselves raises.

ALIFANO: During those years you taught yourself German, didn't you?

BORGES: Yes, it was during the last or next-to-last year of the war. I was seventeen. I owe Carlyle my love for German culture, but I decided to teach myself the German language to read in the original Schopenhauer's *The World as Will and Idea* and also Heine and Goethe.

ALIFANO: You have said on past occasions that one of the persons who encouraged you most to become a writer was your father. What was Jorge Guillermo Borges like? What memories do you have of him?

BORGES: My father was an admirable man in every way. He was a professor of psychology and modern languages. I remember him as a brilliant man, although perhaps somewhat shy. I believe that I inherited my shyness from him. My father taught three courses a week and earned a fairly respectable salary, enough to support his family. Any money left over he spent on books to enrich his library and to give as presents to his students. I believe that in some way he foresaw that I would be a writer, that I had a literary destiny, and he encouraged me to fulfill it. I remember that my father always advised me to write a great deal, never to abandon writing, but to do it only when I felt the need to and, essentially, not to hurry into print, that there was always time enough for that.

ALIFANO: When did you decide to publish your first book, Borges?

BORGES: Well, following my father's advice, I decided to do it after I had written my third or fourth book. That first book was titled (*is* titled) *Fervor de Buenos Aires* (Fervor of Buenos Aires) and was published in 1923. My father paid for the edition; he gave me three hundred pesos for its printing, and I ran full of enthusiasm to a printer. I remember we were about to go to Europe and were forced to finish its production in six days. Then copies were given away among my friends in Buenos Aires. In Spain the distinguished writer Gómez de la Serna praised it in a review; undoubtedly, it was undeserving of such praise.

ALIFANO: In 1926 you were already a well-known poet, and César Tiempo and Pedro-Juan Vignale included your poetry in an anthology of Argentine poetry they edited. A year later you published your second volume of poetry: *Luna de enfrente* (Moon Across the Way).

BORGES: That anthology was entitled *Exposición de la actual poesía argentina* (Showcase of Recent Argentine Poetry), and it took two years to be published. There, in a prologue to my poems, I stated that I was writing another book on the theme of Buenos Aires or, more precisely, on the theme of Palermo, the neighborhood in Buenos Aires where I lived. It was to be entitled simply *Cuaderno San Martín* (San Martín Copybook). It came out in 1929, and I had never imagined that that book of poetry would earn several prizes; among them the Second Municipal Prize for Literature. But if you allow me a brief digression, I will tell you something amusing.

ALIFANO: Please do.

BORGES: Well, in 1930 I received a pleasant surprise: in one year, twenty-seven copies of my book had been sold. I was so moved that I wanted to know the name of each one of my readers so that I could thank them personally for having bought my book. I told this to my mother, and she was very moved. "Twenty-seven books is an incredible amount," she said to me. She added: "You are becoming a famous man, Georgie."

ALIFANO: You just mentioned your mother, Borges, someone I met personally and for whom I had great affection. Can we talk about doña Leonor?

BORGES: My mother was an extraordinary person. I should speak, above all, of her kindness toward me. I'll tell you a secret of mine. I feel somewhat guilty for not having been a happy man in order to have given her a deserved happiness. I feel guilty; perhaps I should have been more understanding of her. But I don't know; I suppose that it is true of all children that when our mother dies, we feel that we have taken her for granted as we do with the moon or the sun or the seasons: we feel we have abused her. Before her death, it doesn't dawn on us. My mother was an intelligent and gracious woman who, I believe, had no enemies. She was a friend to all sorts of people. Sometimes very old black women came to our home to visit her; those women were descendants of slaves who had belonged to my family. One of those black women bore the same name as my mother, Leonor Acevedo. During the nineteenth century some slaves took the name of their masters; that is why that woman had the same name as my mother.

I remember that during the hard years of Perón's dictatorship, when I was expelled from the presidency of the Society of Writers for refusing to hang Perón's portrait in my office, we were threatened by a criminal. The fellow came late at night, and my mother answered the door: "I am going to kill you and your son," said a voice, appropriately harsh and professionally malevolent. "Why?" asked my mother. "Because I am a Peronist," added the unknown man. Then my mother answered him: "Well, if you want to kill my son, it's very easy. He leaves home for his office every morning at eight; all you have to do is wait for him. As for myself, señor, I have turned eighty, and I advise you to hurry up if you want to kill me, because I might very well die on you beforehand."

ALIFANO: An admirably courageous attitude, worthy of doña Leonor . . .

BORGES: How fitting, besides, that "*Yo-me-le-muero-antes*" (I might very well die on you beforehand)! It is said in a delightfully colloquial manner. Now, what a stupid threat! Well, really, all death threats are stupid and ridiculous. In what way can one be threatened other than with death? It would be truly clever or original to threaten someone with immortality!

ALIFANO: The threat was obviously never carried out.

BORGES: No; it never was. I am telling you that anecdote, and my mother died of natural causes nearing her hundredth birthday. Poor mother! She complained that God had kept her alive too long. I remember that when she turned ninety-five, she said to me: "Goodness me, Georgie, I think I overdid it." Every night she would ask God not to wake her the following morning. And then she would wake up and cry; but she didn't complain. There came a night in which God surely heard her, and she died at four in the morning.

ALIFANO: Is it true that your mother had contempt for the *compadritos* (hoodlums) and the *guapos* (the toughs), whom increasingly you included in your work, beginning with your essay on the poet Evaristo Carriego?

BORGES: Yes, she didn't admire them. Once she said to me: "Let it be the last time you write about those coarse men. I am fed up with your hoods. You describe them as though they were brave men, but the *guapos* are nothing but a bunch of bums." My mother didn't like that subject in the least and blamed poor Carriego, who was also fascinated by the cult of courage, for having corrupted me.

ALIFANO: Carriego, who was from your neighborhood, rubbed elbows with the *guapos*, didn't he?

BORGES: Yes, he personally met almost all the criminals of his time. I, on the other hand, also met them, but only when they were somewhat on the sidelines, when they had already retired. I met the *guapo* Nicólas Paredes, for example, when he was very old, and I became a friend of his. The last time I visited him at his house, he gave me a present—an orange. He lived in abject poverty, and before I left, he said: "No one leaves my house empty-handed, Borges." And as he couldn't find anything else to give me, he gave me an orange, which I would have liked to preserve forever.

ALIFANO: And what did your mother think of Evaristo Carriego, who was a friend of your family?

BORGES: She thought he was a good young man, but without any talent. Carriego died in 1912, and in 1930 I published a book-length essay on him. My mother asked me then: "Why did you write a book about that boy?" I explained to her, searching for an excuse, that it was because he had been a neighbor of ours. "But, son," she answered, "if you are going to write a book about each of our neighbors, we are finished."

ALIFANO: You frequently mention the Andalusian writer Rafael Cansinos-Asséns, whom you considered to be your mentor. What memories do you have of him, Borges?

BORGES: Ah, truly great memories. He was one of the last people I saw before I returned from Europe in the 1920s, and it was as though all at once I had come upon all the libraries of the West and of the East. Cansinos-Asséns boasted that he could greet the stars in fourteen classical and modern languages. He was a man who had read all the books in the world; at least that was the impression I had of him whenever we spoke. He translated Barbusse from French, *The Thousand and One Nights* from Arabic. He translated Latin writers and translated an excellent selection of the Talmud directly from Hebrew.

ALIFANO: Did you see Cansinos-Asséns frequently?

BORGES: Yes, quite frequently. I used to attend a *tertulia* (coterie) which he presided over in a coffee house in Madrid. During those years, there were several *tertulias* in Spain; another was the one of Ramón Gómez de la Serna, in the famous Cáfe de Pombo. The painter Gutiérrez Solana, who created a great painting of all the members, used to attend that *tertulia*. I went to it once and didn't care for it; I preferred the *tertulia* of Cansinos-Asséns.

ALIFANO: Cansinos-Asséns was a man of very modest means, wasn't he?

BORGES: Yes. He lived very frugally and earned his living as a translator. He was a man who hardly ever left his library. I remember he had written a very lovely poem on the theme of the sea. When I congratulated him, he answered me in his Andalusian accent: "Yes, yes, the sea surely must be very beautiful. I hope to see it sometime." He had never seen the sea! Like Coleridge, he held the archetype in his imagination and thus had reached an admirable solution.

ALIFANO: Borges, you said that Gómez de la Serna had praised your first book, *Fervor de Buenos Aires*, but a moment ago you said you didn't like the *tertulia* of the Café de Pombo led by the author of *La Nardo*, together with Gutiérrez Solana. Why didn't you like it?

BORGES: I didn't care for it because Gómez de la Serna was a sort of dictator who spoke badly of everybody else. The *tertulia* of Cansinos-Asséns was quite the opposite. There, no one was allowed to speak ill about others. When I attended the *tertulia* of Gómez de la Serna, by his invitation, I was bothered, above all, by a poor wretch who was there, a sort of professional buffoon who came every Saturday wearing a bracelet with rattles on his wrist. Gómez de la Serna had him shake hands with people and then would ask: "Rattle, rattle, where is the serpent?" And all those attending would laugh at that idiocy. That seemed to me very sad. I thought that Gómez de la Serna had no right to use that wretch to play such a cruel joke, which it would be best to forget. When I left (convinced, moreover, that I would never return), Gómez de la Serna said to me: "I am sure that you've never seen anything like this in Buenos Aires." "No, luckily I've never seen anything like it," I answered.

ALIFANO: And yet, what a great writer Gómez de la Serna was! Did you at any time see him as a man of genius?

BORGES: Yes. I have no doubt that he was a man of genius. A great writer with a poetic sense of life, but I believe that he regrettably went astray with those brief utterances or images that he called *Greguerías* and which were like bubbles of thought.

ALIFANO: Do you consider the *Greguerías* a weakness in the work of Gómez de la Serna?

BORGES: Definitely. I am sure that he could have accomplished better work if he had thought in a wider framework. He was the composer of a remarkable prose; along with Alfonso Reyes, he was one of the great prose writers in the history of the Spanish language. Few have mastered the language like Gómez de la Serna, but I insist that he went astray in his obsession with fragmentary thinking. Unfortunately, he had read a book by Jules Renard titled *Regard*, which is written in brief statements. Gómez de la Serna gave his bubbles the name of *Greguerías* and began inventing those atoms of thought. I now remember that Baldomero Fernández Moreno defined the *Greguerías* as "ingenious and ephemeral fancies." And it is true. They are exactly that. In one of those *Greguerías* Gómez de la Serna states, for example, "The fish most difficult to catch in the water is the soap." I see it as an appealing witticism that can surprise, but that is nothing more than a momentary fancy. A metaphor, as I understand it, must gather deeper affinities. And the affinity between a soap and a fish is not interesting in the least. It is more or less like that metaphor of Vicente Huidobro which reads: "The elevators climb like thermometers." Exactly, the elevators climb like a column of mercury, but I don't know if such similarity, somewhat frivolous and trivial, can move anybody, at least it doesn't move me.

ALIFANO: Yes, obviously, it is not an essential metaphor. It may startle us, but it doesn't move us, as you have noted.

BORGES: But if one uses a metaphor such as: "One cannot step twice into the same river," we find that the content is more profound. The idea of a river and of time is an essential association, for we think of time as a river. Time is something that flows and that one cannot imagine otherwise; it is impossible to imagine time as a series of digits or as something static. Time moves. It contains the past and the future; as Browning says, the present is the instant in which the future crumbles into the past. But coming back to metaphors: I think that the similarity between a river and time makes it a true and inevitable metaphor. But if I compare a bar of soap to a fish or an elevator to a thermometer, it gives the impression of something that is used for its mere shock effect and that is foreign to poetic thinking.

ALIFANO: Was the review of your book *Fervor de Buenos Aires* published in a journal in Madrid?

BORGES: No. It was published in a famous magazine: *La Revista de*

Occidente (The Magazine of [the] West)—I never knew why it carried such a name. It should have been called *La Revista del Occidente*; *del* (of the) is the correct form and not *de* (of). But, let's leave it as it is. Ignorance of the Spanish language is unfortunately all too common. But, well, what can we do about it!

ALIFANO: And what is your opinion of the Spanish poet Oliverio Girondo?

BORGES: Girondo was a willfully extravagant man. I think he strove very hard to imitate Gómez de la Serna. I never liked what he wrote. Recently, Mujica Láinez reminded me of some lines that Girondo wrote about Venice which read: "*Bajo los puentes, los gondoleros fornican con la noche*" (Beneath the bridges, the gondoliers make love to the night). What wretchedness! Those lines seem so awful to me.

ALIFANO: So you don't see any brilliance in Oliverio Girondo as you do in Gómez de la Serna?

BORGES: I don't think his best friends could attribute that quality to him.

ALIFANO: Borges, what was Buenos Aires like during the 1920s, when you came back from Europe?

BORGES: It was very exciting. There was a great cultural life, much as in any European country; I was very surprised by it. During those years, culture was a living thing. I remember that in all the cafés there were intriguing characters who created excitement and interest. People also played ingenious practical jokes on each other. I also met the writer and sociologist José Ingenieros, who had his coterie and was famous at the time. He and the novelist Macedonio Fernández played memorable pranks; they had a great sense of humor. I regret to hear that it's not done anymore. It's too bad, don't you think so, Alifano?

ALIFANO: Yes, I agree with you. Particularly that the coteries have disappeared in Buenos Aires. Can we speak a little about your friends, Borges: Who were your friends during those years?

BORGES: Well, the friends I remember most—almost all are now dead, but I can name Enrique Amorim, Francisco Luis Bernárdez, Ernesto Palacio (from whom I later grew apart because he became a follower of Perón), Carlos Mastronardi, Ulyses Petit de Murat, Eduardo Gonzáles Lanuza, Ricardo Molinari, Xul Solar. Dear God, there are so many! I would not want to forget any of them!

ALIFANO: When did you meet Adolfo Bioy Casares?

BORGES: Many years ago, but Adolfito is younger than I am by a few years. What I can't remember is how I came to meet him; even less the date we met, since my dates are always vague. Later I met Silvina Ocampo, and when she married Adolfito on a farm he had in the province of Buenos Aires, I was a witness at the wedding, I and the foreman of the farm.

ALIFANO: Your mutual friendship has benefited literature, since you have collaborated in writing the famous stories by H. Bustos Domecq[1], that strange character who for more than forty years has inhabited the rather small territory of Argentine letters. Also, you and your friend Bioy founded and directed for many years *El Séptimo Circulo* editions, which published in Spanish the most remarkable detective stories from around the world.

BORGES: How strange, isn't it! Silvina Ocampo disliked the Bustos Domecq stories. When Adolfito and I would read them aloud to some of our friends, she would say they were a string of silly things, and she would leave. The truth is, we used to make up those stories to have some fun. Now I am taken aback by the baroque style in which we wrote them.

ALIFANO: And yet Silvina and Bioy together wrote an excellent detective novel, *Los que aman, odian* (Those Who Love, Hate), a good contribution to the genre, in a style not identical to that of the Bustos Domecq stories but still rather similar. Do you remember that novel?

BORGES: Yes. It is very good. It's a shame that Adolfito and Silvina have not written other works together! Silvina is a woman of genius. I would say she is the best Argentine short story writer.

ALIFANO: I completely agree with you. And what is your opinion of Bioy?

BORGES: Bioy Casares is the only classical person I have known. I owe him so much. Adolfito is the least superstitious reader I know, he is immune to all types of fanaticisms; he is a person who professes, perhaps to the outrage of everyone, the cult of Doctor Johnson, of Voltaire and of Confucius. He has written one of the most timeless novels in Argentine literature: a fantastical novel which I was honored to exalt and did not hesitate to label as perfect. I am referring to *La invención de Morel* (The Invention of Morel). I'll tell you something about Adolfito. Sometimes, in his home, he picks up a book and without revealing who the author

[1]Borges and Adolfo Bioy Casares published in 1942, under the pseudonym of H. Bustos Domecq, a volume of detective stories, *Seis Problemas para don Isidro Parodi* (Six Problems for Don Isidro Parodi), in which they parodied the conventions of the genre. In 1946, using the same pseudonym, they published two fantastic short stories: *Dos Fantasías memorables* (Two Memorable Fantasies).

is he reads a few paragraphs aloud to make his guests laugh. Then it turns out that he was reading from one of his first books, *María Merluza la planchadora* (María Merluza the Laundress) or *La estatua casera* (The Domestic Statue). Isn't that amusing?

2

Facing the Year 1983

ALIFANO: How do you usually celebrate
New Year's Eve, Borges?
BORGES: Silently, as time does.

ALIFANO: The approach of a new year usually implies a weighing or summing up of events that have taken place during the old year. How would you sum up 1982, Borges?

BORGES: I believe that everything that has happened during 1982 in our country has been distressing. So that I am not sure whether it is desirable to recall this year. Perhaps it would be better to forget, don't you think so? There were strikes and demonstrations protesting all sort of things; and the military carried out an absurd war in which we did not come out well and in which many young men died. Well, everything was very dark. It seems to me that it is better to forget, even though next year we may remember this one with a certain nostalgia.

ALIFANO: Does that mean that you expect 1983 to be worse?

BORGES: Well, I don't know. But our situation does not seem to suggest anything else. Many people say that I am a pessimist, a man who has lost hope. But how else can one be in these times? Now, of course, if I were given complete power to rule the nation I wouldn't know what to do. I would give it back immediately. How can one stop the corruption? How can one confront the moral crisis in which our country is steeped? How can one reestablish democracy in a country in which such deeds have been done with such impunity? I wouldn't know what to do. Terrible things have happened here and no one has the courage to assume the responsibility for them.

ALIFANO: Borges, you have stated on several occasions that you are against all types of nationalism and that national borders should be abolished on the earth so that every person would be a citizen of the world, "patriots to heaven," as Herman Melville wished. Do you believe that

11

many of the evils we suffer from would then disappear?

BORGES: I believe they would. There is a folly in the world, a folly to which we all adhere. A folly of which I have also been guilty: that misconception is *nationalism* and it has brought many evils. We all think, perhaps too much, of the piece of land where we were born and of the blood our ancestors gave us. I, for example, until recently felt proud of my military ancestors. But I no longer do. I no longer feel proud of them. I will tell you something. When I began to write I was known as the grandson of Colonel Borges. Luckily, Colonel Borges is now seen as my grandfather. But as I was saying, nationalism is the main affliction of our times. In ancient times the Stoics coined a word which, I think, we are still unworthy of; I am referring to the word "cosmopolitanism." I believe we should be citizens of the world or, as Goethe would express it, "*Weltbürger*," which means the same.

ALIFANO: Surely that Stoic expression was unacceptable to the Greeks, for they had the cult of the word "fatherland."

BORGES: Ah, certainly that idea must have seemed very odd to Greek citizens. They were, before everything else, men who came from a city: Xenophanes of Elea, Heraclitus of Ephesus, Alexander of Macedonia. Now, I believe that if we can think of ourselves as citizens of the world, or "patriots to heaven," life in our planet would be better. We love overemphasizing our little differences, our hatreds, and that is wrong. If humanity is to be saved, we must focus on our affinities, the points of contact with all other human beings; by all means we must avoid accentuating our differences.

ALIFANO: Do you remember Quevedo's phrase: "*Me dices que ves mal al mundo; te digo que ves al mundo*" (You tell me you see the world as evil; I tell you that you are seeing the world). It suggests that every era has its share of evils. Perhaps our own is not better or worse than other eras, don't you think?

BORGES: Yes, that may be true. But it seems that ours went overboard. I now remember a dream of Wordsworth's found in the fifth book of *The Prelude*; it is a dream that De Quincey praised highly. This happened at the beginning of the nineteenth century. Wordsworth said that he was very worried by the danger the arts and sciences were in, at the mercy of any cosmic catastrophe. When he expressed his fears to a friend, the friend answered by saying he had often felt the same. Then Wordsworth told him his dream, which seems to me to be a perfect nightmare.

He said that he was in a cave by the seaside, that it was noon, the overwhelming hour of midday lethargy, that he was reading *Don Quixote*, one of his favorite books, and that suddenly sleep overcame him. He fell asleep facing the sea, on the golden sand of the beach. In his dream he is surrounded by a wilderness of black sand. There is no water, there is no sea. He is in the midst of a desert, horrified, trying to escape, when he notices that there is someone beside him. He is an Arab from the Bedouin tribes. He holds a lance in his right hand; under his left arm he has a stone, and in his hand, a shell. The Arab tells Wordsworth that he has come on a mission to save the arts and the sciences, and tells him to place the shell against his ear. It is an extraordinarily beautiful shell. Wordsworth tells us that "In an unknown tongue,/ Which yet I understood," he is given the prophecy: a sort of passionate ode, prophesying that the earth is on the verge of being destroyed by a flood sent by the wrath of God. The Arab corroborates that the flood is nearing. He then shows Wordsworth the stone, which is, strangely, "Euclid's Elements" without ceasing to be a stone. Then he places the shell next to Wordsworth, and the shell is also a book: it is the one that has told him those terrible things.

In the shell, moreover, all the poetry of the world is represented, in-cluding—why shouldn't one suppose it?—Wordsworth's own poem. The Arab tells him, "I must save both of these things, the stone and the shell, both books." Wordsworth looks back and sees the face of the Bedouin changing; it is filled with horror. He looks in the direction the Bedouin is looking and sees a great light, a light that has already flooded half the desert. It is the waters of the flood that will destroy the earth. The Bedouin goes away and Wordsworth sees that the Bedouin is also Don Quixote and and that his camel is also Rocinante, and that in the same way the stone is a book and the shell is a book, the Bedouin is Don Quixote and is neither and both those beings at the same time. This duality is part of the dream's horror. Wordsworth at that point wakes up in despair, screaming with terror. The waters were already reaching him.

ALIFANO: It's true, as you've pointed out, that dream is a perfect night-mare. It contains the two essential elements: the horror of supernatural things and the terror of persecution.

BORGES: Yes, without doubt, it is a model nightmare. At that time, such a dream, the idea that a cosmic catastrophe could destroy the world was very rare. Nowadays, that idea, that dream or nightmare, is very common. Now we can believe that all of humanity's achievements, that humanity itself, can be destroyed at any moment by nuclear bombs. Our destiny is in the hands of irrational individuals! How can we think otherwise? You have seen how, here, in our country, a demagogue summoned people to the Plaza de Mayo and declared war without considering its consequences. Although I've been told that a reporter may be the one to blame. It seems that the president came out from the presidential house and a reporter who was there to interview him told him, "They say that the British will send their navy. If that happens, what will be your decision, Mister President?" The president in turn questioned the reporter, "What would you do?" And the journalist answered: "I would fight them, Mister President." "That is what we'll do," answered the president. Next day the war with England began.

ALIFANO: But despite everything, Borges, and in the midst of such senselessness, as you correctly note, people continue to paint, continue to write poems, they continue, in fact, to create beauty. This beauty, thank God, is everywhere. Do you remember that invocation of your mentor, the Spanish-Jewish poet, Rafael Cansinos-Asséns?

BORGES: Of course, how could I forget it! "Oh, Lord, let there not be so much beauty!" How lovely, isn't it! I thank you for bringing it to mind. It's true, beauty is always pursuing us and it wouldn't be at all strange if we found beauty scattered throughout various languages. I feel guilty for not having given more time to studying the literature of the Orient. All I did was to approach it through translations. But I have felt the power of that beauty. That memorable verse of the Persian poet Hafiz comes to mind: "I fly, my ashes will be what I am." In those brief, precise words the doctrine of the transmigration of souls is expressed. I will be reborn again and again, in another century "my ashes will be what I am."

ALIFANO: It would be wonderful if beauty were a contagious disease, and people, once in a while, would fall sick with beauty, don't you think so, Borges?

BORGES: Yes, it would be wonderful. We would all go about lost, drifting, but it wouldn't matter; surely it would be wonderful. And people would certainly live without hatred. For me to live without hatred is easy since I've never felt hatred.

ALIFANO: But to live without love, I believe is impossible.

BORGES: Fortunately, impossible! I've always been in love with some woman. I don't know, but I believe that love is a divine gift and, like beauty, love also pursues us everywhere. I feel slightly embarrassed to refer to my personal life, but people expect confidences and I have no reason to deny them mine. Love led me to understand my blindness, taught me not to give up. And then my blindness led me to study the Anglo-Saxon language and that richer and more recent world: Scandinavian literature. Later I wrote *Antiguas literaturas germánicas* (Ancient Germanic Literatures). I studied its periods and the sagas, and I wrote poems based on those themes; and, above all, I enjoyed myself.

ALIFANO: Please forgive me, Borges, for asking you this: What is blindness to you?

BORGES: Well, now it is a way of life, a way of life that is not entirely unhappy. A writer—and, I believe, generally all persons—must think that whatever happens to him or her is *a resource*. All things have been given to us for a purpose, and an artist must feel this more intensely. All that happens to us, including our humiliations, our misfortunes, our embarrassments, all is given to us as raw material, as clay, so that we may shape our art.

ALIFANO: Mallarmé said that the world exists so that we may fulfill a book, and earlier, much earlier, Homer had written in the eighth book of *The Odyssey* that "the gods wrought and spun the skein of ruin for men, that there might be a song for those yet to be born."

BORGES: Well, it is the same idea. In one of my poems I say that humiliation, misfortune, discord, were given to us so that we may transmute them, so that we may make from the miserable circumstance of our life eternal works or works that aspire to be so. I believe and feel, for example, that blindness was given to me as a gift. Blindness has given me the affection of many people. People always feel good will toward a blind man. A verse of Goethe's comes to mind. My German is deficient but I'll try to remember the original, *"Alles Nahe wird fern"* (All that is near becomes far). In that verse Goethe was referring not only to the sunset, but also to life. All things leave us. In my case, the visible world has moved away from my eyes, surely forever, but, fortunately, it has been replaced by other things. My duty is to accept and, as far as possible, to enjoy those things.

ALIFANO: Borges, what is your opinion of the festivities that are celebrated at the end of the year?

BORGES: Well, people behave as though the end of the world were coming with the end of each year. It is a collective illusion that is sometimes, or almost always, imbued with a commercial purpose, and of course nothing ever actually happens. De Quincey said that every official celebration is sad, for people are compelled to celebrate. But I believe that happiness is an end in itself, beyond any celebration. Joy is not a matter of making a toast or of exploding fireworks.

ALIFANO: When we started this dialogue I asked you to sum up the year.

Perhaps I should have asked you to speak of your projects.

BORGES: Yes, that would have been better, no doubt. I prefer to speak about projects. I am eighty-three years old, perhaps I may die this very night, but I can tell you some of my projects. For example, next year I hope to visit India; I expect to write another book; I expect to finish, with your help, the translation of Stevenson's fables. Well, just to list all of them would take a long time, and I would have to live until I am one hundred and ten to fulfill all the plans I have.

ALIFANO: How do you usually celebrate New Year's Eve, Borges?

BORGES: Silently, as time does. I go to Bioy Casares's home and there we enjoy it without noise, like one more night—remembering things. And yes—drinking a little *sidra* (hard cider). My friend Xul Solar used to offer advice for New Year's Eve. He used to say that whatever one does that night is what he will do throughout the new year. I have accepted his belief; therefore, most likely tonight I'll write a poem or read some verses so that the prophecy may be fulfilled.

3

Memories of a Trip to Japan

> ... one is a guest in a Japanese house
> and asks, "Is there an atlas in this
> house?" And they answer: "Yes, there
> is." Then they add: "Regrettably we
> do not have an atlas." But they begin
> by agreeing with the guest.

ALIFANO: In 1976, in collaboration with Alicia Jurado, you published
a book entitled *Qué es el Budismo?* (What is Buddhism?), and four years
later you were invited by the Ministry of Education of Japan to visit that
country. Can we talk about the surprises that trip surely must have had
for you, Borges?

BORGES: Yes. I was indeed invited by the Ministry of Education of that
wonderful country. And it came about because of that book I coauthored
with Alicia Jurado. I spent five unforgettable weeks in Japan, where
nothing was demanded of me and I was given everything. They made it
possible for me to know cities, gardens, temples, sunsets, mornings, to talk
with Buddhist monks, with priests, with writers. ... And, as I said, in
exchange for all this, they asked nothing of me; they didn't even set a
schedule for me.

ALIFANO: I imagine that for a person like yourself, who is interested in
all aspects of Oriental culture, each day must have brought a new impression.

BORGES: True, each day created a new impression for me. I had expressed a wish that no events were to be scheduled for me while I was there,
and these marvelous people acceded to my wish completely. So that each
day brought me a new gift. I was the one who proposed: "This morning,"
I would say, "we will go to Nara to contemplate the great statue of Buddha,"
or "This afternoon we will attend a tea ceremony," and they agreed. And I
felt something truly beautiful: the pleasure of being in a truly civilized
country. Although it may seem odd, Japan is the most civilized country
that I've known.

ALIFANO: Can you give an example of that impression, Borges?

BORGES: Yes. And I'll do it by referring to the amazing courtesy of its people. I remember that we visited the great image of Buddha—almost thirty meters tall—with its terrible face. A tourist who was with the group I was with, an American tourist, asked the guide: "This image is made of wood, isn't it?" And the guide answered: "Yes, sir, this image is made of wood." Another tourist, who knew about Japanese courtesy, understood that the question had been formulated incorrectly. (If one asks: "This image is made of wood?" the guide does not disagree, since one is suggesting the wood. To contradict another person is for the Japanese an impertinence that has no place in their culture.) After a prudent time, the other tourist reformulated the question, saying: "What is the image of the Buddha made of?" And the guide answered: "It's made of bronze, sir." The guide could now answer correctly, since the second tourist wasn't suggesting anything; rather, he was posing the question in such a way that a precise answer was possible.

ALIFANO: It is a good example of Japanese courtesy. Doesn't that courtesy preclude all forms of discussion or debate?

BORGES: Ah, of course. The Japanese never argue; they always agree with the other person. Another example: one is a guest in a Japanese house and asks: "Is there an atlas in this house?" And they answer: "Yes, there is." Then they add: "Regrettably we do not have an atlas." But they begin by agreeing with the guest.

ALIFANO: Another remarkable aspect of that legendary country must undoubtedly be the harmonious existence of so many cultures, isn't that so?

BORGES: Well, the identifiable cultural roots are three; the Chinese heritage, the Western heritage, and the Japanese tradition itself. Now, I have noticed that Chinese culture has the greatest weight, and it is the one the Japanese like to emphasize. The Japanese owe China *kanji* and Buddhism. They have preserved the *kanji* or ideograms. In order to read a newspaper, for example, it is necessary to know about five thousand *kanji*. The *kanji* are infinite; I think that nobody knows their total number. A number of them are learned by children in school. But then there are others that have a technical meaning; that is, there are *kanji* that a physician knows, but that a poet or an engineer ignores, and vice versa.

ALIFANO: And our culture, Western culture, has it had much impact on Japan?

BORGES: Yes, very much. And they utilize it perhaps even better than

Westerners themselves. They have adapted all sorts of technical devices and artifacts for comfortable living and have perfected them with admirable practical sense. The musical equipment, cameras, tape recorders, watches, etc., that are manufactured there now worry Western industrial companies because they are taking markets away from them throughout the world. Now, the traditional culture of Japan is, in turn, harmoniously integrated into all other aspects of the country. The Japanese have the wisdom to extract what is of interest to them in other cultures, modifying them and enriching them.

ALIFANO: And as for religion, Borges, how is spiritual coexistence practiced?

BORGES: That is another example of the extraordinary tolerance of the Japanese. Two religions are mainly practiced there: Shintoism and Buddhism. In addition, there are converts to Christianity and to various sects derived from it. Shintoism is the ancient religion of Japan. It is a kind of pantheism with eight million deities who travel the whole world entering one object, then another. So everything is sacred and has a divine life. Buddhism came to Japan from India, but by way of China. It is divided into several sects, Zen being the best known. All those religions coexist harmoniously and with absolute tolerance.

ALIFANO: Can you tell me something about the poetry of Japan and its forms which have had such a great influence on us Westerners?

BORGES: The Japanese have achieved a wise ambiguity in their poetry. And that, I believe, is because of their particular form of writing itself, because of the possibilities that their ideograms present. Each one, according to its features, can have several connotations. Take, for example, the word "gold." This word represents or suggests autumn, the color of leaves, or the sunset because of its yellow color.

ALIFANO: So the connotation of each word is multiple and diverse.

BORGES: Yes. The *kanji* allow that ambiguity. And then there are the poetical forms. The classical Japanese poem is the *tanka*, which is made up of five lines divided into two stanzas, one of three lines and the other of two. The structure of the *tanka* led to the *renga*, which is a sequence of *tankas* generally written by different poets. The *renga*, in turn, in the sixteenth century, adopted an ingenious form that was called *haikai*, and that later became what is now called *haiku*. I have written *tankas*, and I have tried to adhere to the metric rules of the form; I have also written *haiku*, which is more difficult, since it only has three lines of five, seven and five syllables. I have practiced those literary forms, but I don't know whether my *tankas* and my *haiku* would sound like those forms to an Oriental ear. Possibly they would not, because I don't think that the *haiku* permits elision or a differentiation between accents that fall on the penultimate or last syllable. So I am not sure how they have turned out.

ALIFANO: I don't know if José Juan Tablada, the Mexican poet who most used those forms in Spanish America, observed such rules. I understand that Japan's traditional poetic forms are guided by strict and, in a certain way, aristocratic esthetics. Perhaps that wise ambiguity, which you noted, together with our ignorance of the *kanji*, or of Japanese, is the greatest obstacle for Westerners who try to imitate that literary genre. Do you think so?

BORGES: Yes, I agree with you. I remember that a *haiku* by Bashô reads: "The dry branch/ crow/ autumn nightfall." If we analyze it we find an extraordinary ambiguity, a magical ambiguity. A crow has perched on a branch, and we don't know if he is one or many crows. The word "nightfall," in turn, is also suggestive. The reader is left to choose among many possibilities implicit in the word. In each *haiku*, besides, one must refer to a precise season of the year. Now, this can be done indirectly, since one can speak of autumn without mentioning autumn but by mentioning rain instead.

ALIFANO: So it's possible to use a symbol for each concept?

BORGES: That's right. Each thing can be symbolized by another. You mentioned José Juan Tablada, but he did not, I believe, adhere to those rules. I think that his attempt was independent of them. Antonio Machado also tried this genre, but he did so with a different attitude. More precisely, he echoed Japanese authors.

ALIFANO: Borges, your thoughts about Japanese poetical forms and your interest in practicing them lead me to ask you this question: Would you dare to learn the Japanese language?

BORGES: Well, I don't know if at eighty-three a man can dare to learn anything, but I've been told that it is not too difficult. Yes, I believe that I could learn Japanese. Now, what would be more difficult for me, undoubtedly, would be to write it. It would be impossible at my late age, because of my blindness, to learn so many *kanji*. As far as its phonetics, it is quite similar to ours, except for two sounds which are almost impossible to reproduce in our language. While I was in Japan, I heard that the Japanese pronounced such words as Buenos Aires, Montevideo, España, in a fashion similar to our own. Their difficulty is that they cannot pronounce the letter *l*. The pronunciation of all other words by a Japanese is not different from the way an Argentine would say them; they are, however, different from the way that an Englishman or a Frenchman would pronounce them.

ALIFANO: The attraction Japan has for you is also what led you to write the story you entitled *"El incivil maestro de ceremonias Kotsuké no Suke"* (The Uncivil Master of Ceremonies Kotsuké no Suke), which is in your book, *La historia universal de la infamia* (A Universal History of Infamy). Isn't that so, Borges?

BORGES: Yes. In that story I retell the famous legend of the lord of the castle of Akō and his forty-seven loyal *rōnin* who commit suicide at the tomb of their offended lord.

ALIFANO: Did you visit his tomb?

BORGES: Yes, of course. I could not have done otherwise. It was one of the things that I had imposed upon myself as a duty during my trip to Japan. I was there with a Buddhist monk who revealed details to me I hadn't known before.

ALIFANO: When was that legend created, Borges?

BORGES: At the beginning of the eighteenth century. But I have not been the only one to treat its theme in a story. About a hundred novels, several plays, and thousands of doctoral theses commemorate that legend, I don't know exactly. One would also have to add its representation in film and in folk art—in porcelain and in lapis lazuli—which tell it through their images. I took it from Mitford and, like him, I concerned myself with the events of the glorious episode and not its local color, which I tried to avoid as much as possible since that has been depicted in several Japanese films inspired by that worthy didactic legend.

ALIFANO: I imagine that in Japan you had the chance to speak intimately with Buddhist monks?

BORGES: Yes, I did. And it was very satisfying to me since I am so interested in that religion. I did it through interpreters but always in an open manner, direct and sincere. I touched upon all the themes I was interested in, and I received extensive and precise answers. But there is a particular dialogue which is worth relating; one I had with a thirty-three-year-old nun who had entered the convent at seventeen. I asked her at some point: "Have you ever regretted having taken the holy orders?" And she answered me, "No. Hardly ever." That "hardly ever" suggested a great sincerity, because she could have answered, "No. I have found my happiness here." But she didn't say that; she said, "Hardly ever," and I was greatly impressed.

ALIFANO: I understand Buddhism does not impose an excessively rigid practice on its monks and nuns; is that correct?

BORGES: No, it doesn't. There is a broad outlook, great liberty and great humility in those people. The Buddhist monks and nuns can abandon their vows whenever they wish. In some instances they can even get married. In Eastern religions, in contrast to our own, they don't uphold the idea of imposing faith by means of the sword. That is an idea completely foreign to the Buddhists.

ALIFANO: Did you attend any performances, Borges?

BORGES: Well, I attended a Kabuki play. It was a presentation of traditional Japanese music and dance. At the beginning, I confess, it seemed to me unbearable, especially the music, in which one cannot make out any melody, and also because the voices of the singers sound very much like a Gregorian choir; but, above all, because of its slowness. An actor, for example, has to lower his hand, which is raised, and he takes five minutes to do so. All that, undoubtedly, has been carefully practiced and follows a tradition. When we found our place, I said to my companion: "Let's stay to see only one show," because I thought I was going to be royally bored. But soon I started to get used to it, and finally I ended up attending the complete festival, which lasted, I believe, six or seven hours. During that time in the theater, one couldn't even hear a fly; and the people, who generally can read music, attentively followed the program that was handed out when they came in. I am blind, and I remember that as I went in, I exclaimed, "Goodness, we are the only ones here." "No," my companion answered, "the room is full, Señor Borges." Nobody speaks loudly there. There may be a crowd, but if one doesn't see, as is my case, he may think that he is alone. Unquestionably, Japan is a civilized country; the most civilized I've ever known.

4

The Labyrinth and the Tiger

I believe that in the idea of the labyrinth
there is also hope, or salvation.

And now that I am blind, one single
color remains for me, and it is precisely
the color of the tiger, the color yellow.

ALIFANO: Borges, I would like to talk with you about two images which
seem to obsess you and which you repeat throughout your work. I am
referring to labyrinths and to the figure of the tiger. I suggest we start with
the former. How did labyrinths enter your literary work; what fascinates
you about them?

BORGES: Well, I discovered the labyrinth in a book published in France
by Garnier that my father had in his library. The book had a very odd
engraving that took a whole page and showed a building that resembled an
amphitheater. I remember that it had cracks and seemed tall, taller than
the cypresses and the men that stood around it. My eyesight was not
perfect—I was very myopic—but I thought that if I used a magnifying
glass, I would be able to see a minotaur within the building. That labyrinth
was, besides, a symbol of bewilderment, a symbol of being lost in life. I
believe that all of us, at one time or another, have felt that we are lost, and I
saw in the labyrinth the symbol of that condition. Since then, I have held
that vision of the labyrinth.

ALIFANO: Borges, what has always intrigued me about labyrinths is not
that people get lost within them, but rather that they are constructions
intentionally made to confound us. Don't you think that this concept
is odd?

BORGES: Yes, it is a very odd idea, the idea of envisioning a builder of
labyrinths, the idea of an architect of labyrinths is indeed odd. It is the idea
of the father of Icarus, Daedalus, who was the first builder of a labyrinth—

the labyrinth of Crete. There is also Joyce's conception, if we are looking for a more literary figure. I have always been puzzled by the labyrinth. It is a very strange idea, an idea which has never left me.

ALIFANO: Various forms of labyrinths appear in your stories. Labyrinths placed in time, like the one of "The Garden of Forking Paths," where you tell about a lost labyrinth.

BORGES: Ah, yes, I do speak of a lost labyrinth in it. Now, a lost labyrinth seems to me to be something magical, and it is because a labyrinth is a place where one loses oneself, a place (in my story) that in turn is lost in time. The idea of a labyrinth which disappears, of a lost labyrinth, is twice as magical. That story is a tale which I imagined to be multiplied or forked in various directions. In that story the reader is presented with all the events leading to the execution of a crime whose intention the reader does not understand. I dedicated that story to Victoria Ocampo. . .

ALIFANO: Do you conceive the image of losing ourselves in a labyrinth as a pessimistic view of the future of mankind?

BORGES: No, I don't. I believe that in the idea of the labyrinth there is also hope, or salvation; if we were positively sure the universe is a labyrinth, we would feel secure. But it may not be a labyrinth. In the labyrinth there is a center: that terrible center is the minotaur. However, we don't know if the universe has a center; perhaps it doesn't. Consequently, it is probable that the universe is not a labyrinth but simply chaos, and if that is so, we are indeed lost.

ALIFANO: Yes, if it didn't have a center, it wouldn't be a cosmos but chaos. Do you believe that the universe may have a secret center?

BORGES: I don't see why not. It is easy to conceive that it has a center, one that can be terrible, or demonic, or divine. I believe that if we think in those terms unconsciously we are thinking of the labyrinth. That is, if we believe there is a center, somehow we are saved. If that center exists, life is coherent. There are events which surely lead us to think that the universe is a coherent structure. Think, for example, of the rotation of the planets, the seasons of the year, the different stages in our lives. All that leads us to believe that there is a labyrinth, that there is an order, that there is a secret center of the universe, as you have suggested, that there is a great architect who conceived it. But it also leads us to think that it may be irrational, that logic cannot be applied to it, that the universe is unexplainable to us, to mankind—and *that* in itself is a terrifying idea.

ALIFANO: All those aspects of the labyrinth fascinated you then?

BORGES: Yes, all of them. But I have also been attracted by the very word *labyrinth*, which is a beautiful word. It derives from the Greek *labyrinthos*, which initially denoted the shafts and corridors of a mine and that now denotes that strange construction especially built so that people would get lost. Now the English word *maze* is not as enchanting or powerful as the Spanish word *laberinto*. *Maze* also denotes a dance, in which the dancers weave a sort of labyrinth in space and time. Then we find *amazement, to be amazed, to be unamazed*, but I believe that *labyrinth* is the essential word, and it is the one I am drawn to.

ALIFANO: Let's go on to the other image: the image of the tiger. Why do you, in choosing an animal, usually choose the image of the tiger?

BORGES: Chesterton said that the tiger was a symbol of terrible elegance. What a lovely phrase, don't you think so? The tiger's terrible elegance.... Well, when I was a child and was taken to the zoo, I used to stop for a long time in front of the tiger's cage to see him pacing back and forth. I liked his natural beauty, his black stripes and his golden stripes. And now that I am blind, one single color remains for me, and it is precisely the color of the tiger, the color yellow. For me, things may be red, they may be blue; the blues may be green, etc., but the yellow is the only color that I see. That is why, since it is the color I see most clearly, I have used it many times and I have associated it with the tiger.

ALIFANO: You must have derived from that the title of one of your books of poems, *The Gold of the Tigers*. Am I right?

BORGES: Yes, that is right. And in the last poem of that book, which has the same title as the book, I speak of the tiger and the color yellow.

> Until the hour of yellow dusk
> How often I looked
> At the mighty tiger of Bengal
> Coming and going in his set path
> Behind the iron bars,
> Unsuspecting they were his jail.
> Later, other tigers came to me,
> Blake's burning tyger;
> Then, other golds came to me,
> Zeus's golden and loving metal,
> The ring that after nine nights
> Gives birth to nine new rings and these, to nine more,
> In endless repetition.
> As the years passed
> The other colors left me
> And now I am left with
> The faint light, the inextricable shadow

And the gold of my beginnings.
Oh dusks, tigers, radiance
Out of myths and epics.
Oh and even a more desired gold, your hair
That my hands long to hold.[1]

ALIFANO: It is a great poem, Borges! I feel that through it you express, in a "light, winged and sacred" way (forgive me for using Plato's words), your fascination with tigers and the color yellow.

BORGES: In the poem I also mention sunsets, which are another frequent theme of my writings and which I see as yellow, in any case they seem to me to be yellow. For that reason for many years I wore yellow ties, which shocked my friends. Some considered them too bright, but to me they were not that bright. They were barely visible. I remember now Oscar Wilde's joke when he said to a friend, "Only a deaf man could wear such a bright tie so shamelessly!" What is even more odd is that when I told this anecdote to a lady, she said: "And why don't you listen to what people say about your tie?" She proved to be much more extreme than Wilde, don't you think?

[1] *Hasta la hora del ocaso amarillo/ Cuántas veces habré mirado/ Al poderoso tigre de Bengala/ Ir y venir por el predestinado camino/ Detrás de los barrotes de hierro,/ Sin sospechar que eran su cárcel./ Después vendrían otros tigres./ El tigre de fuego de Blake;/ Después vendrían otros oros./ El metal amoroso que era Zeus,/ El anillo que cada nueve noches/ Engendra nueve anillos y estos, nueve,/ Y no hay un fin./ Con los años fueron dejándome/ Los otros hermosos colores/ Y ahora sólo me quedan/ La vaga luz, la inextricable sombra/ Y el oro del principio./Oh ponientes, oh tigres, oh fulgores/ Del mito y de la épica,/ Oh un oro más precioso, tu cabello/ Que ansían estas manos.*

5

Funes and Insomnia

> All I did was to write down "Funes"
> instead of "Borges."

ALIFANO: Borges, I am interested to know the circumstances that led you to write that wonderful story, "Funes the Memorious." Could we talk about that strange character who compensates for his deficiencies with his extraordinary memory. Is it true that it relates to a period of insomnia you suffered?

BORGES: Yes, it is true. And I can remember in great detail the circumstances under which I wrote that story. During a time that I had to spend in a hotel, throughout the day I feared the coming of night, because I knew that it was going to be a night of insomnia, that each time I dozed my sleep would be interrupted by atrocious nightmares. I knew that hotel very well; I had lived there as a child. The building has already disappeared; its architecture was full of all the images of the labyrinth. I remember the many patios, the corridors, the statues, the gate, the vast deserted halls, the huge main door, the other entrance doors, the carriage house, the eucalyptus trees, and even a small labyrinth built there. And I particularly remember a clock that punctuated my insomnia, for it inexorably struck every hour: the half hour, the quarter hour and the full hour. So I had no way of deceiving myself. The clock acted as a witness with its metallic ticktock.

I remember that I used to lie down and try to forget everything, and that led me, inevitably, to recall everything. I imagined the books on the shelves, the clothes on the chair, and even my own body on the bed; every detail of my body, the exact position in which my body lay. And so, since I could not erase memory, I kept thinking of those things, and also thinking: if only I could forget, I would certainly be able to sleep. Then

I would recall the belief that when one sleeps, one becomes everyone, or, better said, one is no one, or if one is oneself, one sees oneself in the third person. One is, as Addison said, the actual theater, the spectators, the actors, the author of the drama, the stage—everything simultaneously.

ALIFANO: Forgetfulness would have been a way to free yourself and to fall asleep?

BORGES: Yes. But my insomnia prevented that, and I kept on thinking: continuously imagining the hotel, thinking of my body and of things beyond my body and the hotel. I would think of the adjoining streets, of the street leading to the train station, of the neighboring houses, of the tobacco shop . . . . Later I reached this conclusion: it is fortunate my memory is fallible, fortunate my memory is not infinite. How terrifying it would be if my memory were infinite! It would undoubtedly be monstrous! In that case I would remember every detail of every day of my life, which of course amounts to thousands—as Joyce showed in *Ulysses*. Each day countless things happen, but fortunately we forget them, and furthermore, many of them are repetitions. And so, from that situation I derived the notion of a person who no longer embodied the traditional definition of human faculties (that is, memory and will)—an individual who possessed only memory. Thus, I came upon the idea of that unfortunate country boy, and this was the birth of the story "Funes the Memorious."

ALIFANO: One of the most admirable parables on insomnia ever written.

BORGES: Well, I don't fully agree with your judgment, but there it is! Now, I will reveal something to you that perhaps would be interesting to psychologists. It is strange that after having written that story—after having described that horrible perfection of memory, which ends up destroying its possessor—the insomnia which had distressed me so much disappeared.

ALIFANO: So that the completion of that fantastic tale had a therapeutic effect on you. There are many people who assert that that story is autobiographical; it certainly is, since it is sort of an elaboration of a mental state of yours. Do you agree?

BORGES: Yes. All I did was to write down "Funes" instead of "Borges." I have omitted some aspects of myself and, obviously, I have added others that I don't possess. For example, Funes, the country boy, could not have written the story; I, on the other hand, have been able to write it and to forget Funes and also—though not always—that unpleasant insomnia. Now, I believe that that story is powerful because the reader feels that it is not simply a fantasy, but rather that I am relating something that can happen to him or her, and that happened to me when I wrote it. The entire story comes to be a sort of metaphor, or as you pointed out, a parable of insomnia.

ALIFANO: One notes, moreover, a definite concreteness throughout the story. That is, the character is placed in a specific location and his drama unfolds there.

BORGES: I believe that I succeeded in making "Funes the Memorious" a concrete story. Yes, it does take place in a specific location; that location is Fray Bentos in Uruguay. When I was a child, I spent some time there, in the home of one of my uncles; so I do have childhood memories of the place. Then I chose a very simple character, a simple country boy. As I had to justify his condition in some way, I described a fall from a horse. Really, there are a number of little novelistic inventions that do not harm anyone. Finally, I entitled the story "Funes el memorioso"; a title that suits the story.

ALIFANO: Borges, in English, "Funes the Memorious" must sound odd since the word "memorious" does not exist.

BORGES: True, that word does not exist in English, and it does give the story a grotesque character, an extravagant character. On the other hand, in Spanish—although I don't know if anyone has used the word "memorioso"—if one heard a man from the country say: "Fulano es muy memorioso" (that fellow is very memorious), one would certainly understand him. So that, as I said, I think that the original title goes well with the story. Now, if one seeks an equivalent in another language, for example in French, by using the word "memorié" or some other similar word, the reader is led to see it as a mental state. Thus this title evokes the story of a very simple and unfortunate character killed at an early age by insomnia.

6

Books

I still continue pretending that I am
not blind, I still buy books ... I still
go on filling my house with books.

ALIFANO: There is a theme I would like us to speak about: the theme of
books. I know that it is one of your obsessions. I would be interested to
hear your opinions on the subject.

BORGES: Well, last night, in fact, I had a very strange dream. I dreamed of
the burning of a great library—which I believe may have been the library of
Alexandria—with its countless volumes attacked by flames. Do you
believe this dream may have some meaning?

ALIFANO: Perhaps, Borges. Could it be that you owe your readers a
book on the history of the book? Have you ever thought of writing such
a book?

BORGES: Dear me, no! But it is an excellent idea. It would be wonderful
to write a history of the book. I'll keep it in mind; although I don't know if
an eighty-three-year-old man can set such a project for himself. I don't
know if I am qualified, and to be qualified for such a task is no easy matter;
but, in any case, that work should not be approached merely as a physical
labor. I, for one, am not much interested in the physical nature of books;
particularly in bibliographical books, which are generally excessively long.
I am interested in the various appreciations a book has received. However,
I now remember that Spengler, in his *Decline of the West*, predates my
attempt, for in it he writes remarkable comments on books.

ALIFANO: Well, you have also written some remarkable commentary on
books. I remember the essay "*El culto de los libros*" (The Cult of Books)
in your book *Otras inquisiciones* (Other Inquisitions), where you synthe-
size much of your opinions on the subject; and I also remember a poem

31

entitled "Alexandria, 641 A.D.," which refers precisely to the library of Alexandria and to the caliph Omar, who burned it.

BORGES: Ah, yes, in that poem I conceived the notion of having the caliph express things which most likely he never did; for he was a caliph, and a caliph would not have expressed himself thus. But, thank God, poetry (generally all literature) allows such a thing, and so why couldn't we imagine the caliph speaking. He imagines that the library of Alexandria is the memory of the world; in the vast library of Alexandria everything is found. And then Omar orders the library burned, but he thinks that is unimportant, and says: "*Si de todos / No quedara uno solo, volverían / A engendrar cada hoja y cada línea, / Cada trabajo y cada amor de Hércules, / Cada lección de cada manuscrito.*" (If of all these books / None remained, men would, once again, / Engender each page, each line, / All labor and all of Hercules's love, / Each reading of each manuscript.) In other words, if all the past is in the library, the entire past came from the imagination of men. That is why I believe that beyond its rhetorical virtue, if a work truly possesses it, each generation rewrites anew the books of earlier generations. The differences are found in the cadence, in the syntax, in the form; but we are always repeating the same fables and rediscovering the same metaphors. So that, in some respects, I concur with the caliph Omar—not the historical one, but the caliph I sketched in my poem.

ALIFANO: Nowadays, you must have noticed it, there is a cult of books; a cult which the ancients didn't have. What are the reasons for it, Borges?

BORGES: I believe there are two reasons. First, that all the great masters of mankind, curiously, have been oral; and second, that the ancients saw in the book a substitute for the oral word. I recall a phrase which is often quoted: "*Scripta manent verba volant*" (The written word stays, the spoken word flies). That phrase doesn't mean that the spoken word is ephemeral, but rather that the written word is something lasting and dead. The spoken word, it seems to me now, is somewhat winged and light— "something winged, light and sacred," Plato said in defining poetry. I think that we can apply that concept to the spoken word.

But let's recall another case. The case of Pythagoras, who never wrote so as not to tie himself to the written word, surely because he felt that writing kills and the spoken word fills with life. That is why Aristotle never speaks of Pythagoras but of the Pythagoreans. Pythagoras wished that beyond his physical death his disciples would keep his thoughts alive. Later came that often-quoted Latin phrase: "*Magister dixit*" (The master has said). Which does not mean that the Master has imposed his opinions on his disciples; it means that the disciples continue to expound on the ideas, but if someone opposes them, they invoke: "the Master has said." That phrase is a sort of formula to find reaffirmation and thus to continue professing the ideas of the Master. Speaking of the Pythagoreans, Aristotle tells us that they professed a belief in the dogma of the eternal recurrence, which, somewhat belatedly, Nietzsche would discover.

ALIFANO: That idea of the eternal recurrence or of cyclical time was refuted by Saint Augustine in his *City of God*, do you remember it?

BORGES: Yes. Saint Augustine says, in a beautiful metaphor, that the Cross of Christ saves us from the circular labyrinth of the Stoics. That idea of cyclical time was also touched upon by Hume, Blanqui and others.

ALIFANO: In one of your essays you quote the words of Bernard Shaw. When asked if he truly believed that the Holy Spirit had written the Bible, Shaw answered: "Every book worth being reread has been written by the spirit."

BORGES: Ah, yes. I completely concur with that notion, since a book goes beyond its author's intention. *Don Quixote*, for example, is more than a simple chivalric novel or the satire of a genre. It is an absolute text totally unaffected by chance. The author's intention is a meager human thing, a fallible thing. In a book—in every book—there is a need for something more, which is always mysterious. When we read an ancient book, it is as though we were reading all time that has passed from the day it was written to our present day. A book can be full of errors, we can reject its author's opinions, disagree with him or her, but the book always retains something sacred, something mortal, something magical which brings happiness. In opposition to Macedonio Fernández, who asserted that beauty was something exclusive or given to certain chosen people, I believe that beauty can be found in all things. It would be very strange, for example, if in a book by a Thai poet (I have no knowledge of that country's literature) we could not find a line of poetry that astounds us.

ALIFANO: Borges, you have also asserted that books grow with time, and that the readers themselves modify them and enrich them.

BORGES: Certainly. Books are altered by their readers. For example, the gaucho epic, *Martín Fierro*, that we read now is not the same one written by its author, José Hernández, but rather the one read by Leopoldo Lugones, who undoubtedly enriched it. Similarly, in regard to *Don Quixote* or *Hamlet*; *Hamlet* is also the play that Goethe and Coleridge and Bradley read and interpreted. That is why I feel it is useful that we should maintain a cult of books, since books are a living thing in constant growth.

ALIFANO: In certain ways you profess that cult of books, isn't that so, Borges?

BORGES: Yes, I do. I will tell you a secret. I still continue pretending that I am not blind, I still buy books—you know that very well, I still go on filling my house with books. I feel the friendly gravitational force of the book. I don't exactly know why I believe that a book brings to us a possibility of happiness. A few months ago I was given a marvelous edition of the *Brockhaus Encyclopedia*; and the presence of twenty volumes with beautiful maps and engravings, printed in, I am sure, a no less beautiful Gothic type—that I cannot read—filled me with joy. Those books, almost sacred to me, were there, and I felt their pleasant companionship. Well, I do have a cult of books, I admit it; perhaps this may seem somewhat pathetic, but it is not so. It is something genuine, something sincere and truthful.

ALIFANO: Borges, there are people who speak of the disappearance of books, and they assert that modern developments in communications will replace them with something more dynamic that will require less time than reading. What do you think of that?

BORGES: I believe that books will never disappear. It is impossible that that will happen. Among the many inventions of man, the book, without a doubt, is the most astounding: all the others are extensions of our bodies. The telephone, for example, is the extension of our voice; the telescope and the microscope are extensions of our sight; the sword and the plow are extensions of our arms. Only the book is an extension of our imagination and memory.

ALIFANO: What you have just said brings to mind that Bernard Shaw, in *Caesar and Cleopatra*, refers to the library of Alexandria as the memory of mankind.

BORGES: Yes, I remember that also. And besides being the memory of mankind, it is also its imagination and, why not, its dreams, since it is absurd to suppose that only the waking moments of men engendered the countless pages of countless books.

ALIFANO: Well, you state in a memorable passage that literature is a dream.

BORGES: It is true. Literature is a dream, a controlled dream. Now, I believe that we owe literature almost everything we are and what we have been, also what we will be. Our past is nothing but a sequence of dreams. What difference can there be between dreaming and remembering the past? Books are the great memory of all centuries. Their function, therefore, is irreplaceable. If books disappear, surely history would disappear, and man would also disappear.

7

Poetry

Certain sundowns, certain dawns,
some weathered faces are at the point
of revealing something to us, and this
imminence of a revelation which is not
fulfilled is, for me, the aesthetic act.

ALIFANO: Borges, what is poetry? How would you define it?

BORGES: I believe that poetry is something so intimate, so essential, that it cannot be defined without oversimplifying it. It would be like attempting to define the color yellow, love, the fall of leaves in the autumn. I don't know how essential things can be defined. It seems to me that the only possible definition would be Plato's, precisely because it is not a definition, but a poetic act. When he refers to poetry he says: "That light substance, winged and sacred." That, I believe, can define poetry to a certain extent, since it doesn't confine it to a rigid mold, but rather offers to our imagination the image of an angel or of a bird.

ALIFANO: So that in concurring with Plato's definition, you would accept the idea that poetry is, above all, an aesthetic act?

BORGES: Yes. I still believe that poetry is *the* aesthetic act; that poetry is not the poem, for the poem may be nothing more than a series of symbols. Poetry, I believe, is the poetic act that takes place when the poet writes it, when the reader reads it, and it always happens in a slightly different manner. When the poetic act takes place, it seems to me that we become aware of it. Poetry is a magical, mysterious, unexplainable—although not incomprehensible—event. If one doesn't feel the poetic event upon reading it, the poet has failed.

ALIFANO: Well, but the reader can also fail, don't you think?

BORGES: Ah, yes, that happens frequently, and is more common.

ALIFANO: So the justification of a poem would come after the event, Borges?

BORGES: Certainly. We first feel emotion, and then we explain it or try to explain it. At the same time, for poetry to move us we must feel that it corresponds to an emotion. That is, if we read the poem as a linguistic exercise, if we believe that poetry is a mere word game, poetry fails. I would say, rather, that poetry is expressed in words, but words are not the substance of poetry. The substance of poetry—if I may use the metaphor—is emotion. And that emotion must be shared by the reader.

ALIFANO: What you have just said suggests that the only criterion for poetry is its affective quality, a hedonistic criterion, isn't it?

BORGES: Yes! If a text gives us pleasure, moves us, that text is poetic. If it doesn't move us, it is a wasted effort to point out to us that it has novel rhymes, that the metaphors are unique to the author's style or that they fall within a certain poetic movement. All that is worthless. I'll reveal a personal secret to you: all my life I've repeated those lines by Quevedo which read: "*Su tumba son de Flandres las campañas/ y su epitafio la sangrienta luna*" (His tomb is the campaign of Flanders/ His epitaph the blood-stained moon). My imagination was taken by those lines, but some time ago I wondered: Can we justify that line, "His epitaph the blood-stained moon." Because—and I don't believe this is nonsense—we can also conceive of a moon as the moon of astronomy or as the moon in the Ottoman flag; so it is hard for us to accept that line logically. But perhaps the least important thing is that our logic accepts it as long as our imagination does. We feel that the moon, in this instance, shines bloody over the battlefields, like the red moon of the Apocalypse.

ALIFANO: True. Besides, we feel that there is something magical in those lines.

BORGES: Yes, and the word "epitaph" cannot be replaced by any other, since it is an essential word that speaks for itself. Moreover, I feel the same is true of the word "moon." I don't know whether logically we can justify the word "epitaph," but I believe that the essential thing is that each one of us feels that Quevedo wrote those lines with sincerity, and that we are convinced that those words came naturally to him. Otherwise we would feel that the lines have no power; since that doesn't happen in this case, the poetic act survives and Quevedo's sonnet is full of magic, something mysterious, marvelous.

ALIFANO: Borges, this also suggests that what is important in the art of poetry is finding the precise words.

BORGES: To a great extent. Those precise words are what elicit the emotion. I always remember that wonderful line in a poem by Emily

Dickinson, which can exemplify this: "This quiet dust was gentlemen and ladies." The idea is banal. The idea of dust, the dust of death (we will all be dust one day), is a cliché; but what surprises is the phrase "gentlemen and ladies," which gives the line its magic and poetic quality. If she had written "men and women," it would have failed as poetry; it would have been trivial. But, finding the precise words, she wrote, "This quiet dust was gentlemen and ladies."

ALIFANO: The Argentine poet Lugones believed the essential element is the metaphor. What is your view on this, Borges?

BORGES: I think Lugones is mistaken. For me what is important is the intonation, the cadence in which the metaphor is set. For example, if we say: "Life is a dream," it is a phrase which is too abstract to be poetry, since it is cold, trivial. On the other hand, if we say, as Shakespeare did, "We are such stuff as dreams are made on," that is closer to poetry. However, when Walther von der Vogelweide says, "I have dreamed my life, was it real?" the poetic condition reaches further than in Calderón or Shakespeare. Similarly, in the dream of Chuang Tzu that reads: "Chuang Tzu dreamt he was a butterfly and when he awoke he did not know if he was a man who had dreamt he was a butterfly or a butterfly that was dreaming it was a man." There is poetry in that brief text. The choice of the butterfly is felicitous, since the butterfly has a tenuous quality that is fitting for the stuff of dreams. If Chuang Tzu had instead chosen a tiger, the effect would have changed and that text would not seem poetic to us.

ALIFANO: One of the most beautiful definitions of the aesthetic act comes from you, Borges. In one of your essays you state: "The aesthetic act is the imminence of a revelation which is never fulfilled."

BORGES: Ah, yes, I did say that. It's true. Certain sundowns, certain dawns, some weathered faces are at the point of revealing something to us, and this imminence of a revelation which is not fulfilled is, for me, the aesthetic act. Now, language itself is also an aesthetic creation. I believe this is indisputable; a proof is that when we study a foreign language, when we are compelled to look at words closely, as though with a magnifying glass, we see them either as beautiful or not. This doesn't happen with one's own language, since we see and feel our words as integral to our expression.

ALIFANO: You have said that metaphors exist from our very beginnings. Could you expound on that concept, Borges?

BORGES: Yes, certainly. I believe that metaphors, if they are truly metaphors, exist from the beginning of time. I don't believe it is easy to invent them or to discover affinities that have not already been perceived. But we express them differently. I have occasionally thought of reducing all metaphors to five or six which seem to me to be the essential metaphors.

ALIFANO: What are those metaphors?

BORGES: Well, time and a river; life and dreams; death and sleep; stars and eyes; flowers and women. These would be, I believe, the essential metaphors that are found in all literatures; and then there are others that are whimsical. I believe that the poet's task is to discover metaphors, even though they may already exist. I think that a metaphor doesn't come to a poet as a revelation of a similarity between two disparate things: a metaphor is revealed to the poet in its wholeness, in its form, in its intonation. I don't think that Emily Dickinson thought: "This quiet dust was men and women," and that afterward she changed the latter phrase to "gentlemen and ladies"; that seems unlikely to me. It is more likely that all this was given to her by someone—whom we could call the spirit, the muse—as a single event, at a single time. I don't believe that one arrives at poetry by means of progressions, by searching for all possible variations of words. I believe that one comes upon the proper adjective or adjectives. I remember a verse by Rafael Obligado which reads, "*Estalla el cóncavo trueno*" (the concave thunder bursts). And I am sure that he didn't arrive at such an expression by trying several adjectives accented on the antepenultimate syllable; I think he came directly upon the word "*cóncavo*," which is the precise word, the word we feel as proper, and it is the one that gives the verse its beauty.

ALIFANO: Bradley has said that one of the impressions that poetry should leave us with is not that we are discovering something new, but rather that we are remembering something forgotten.

BORGES: Ah, yes. I didn't remember that, but it supports what I expressed previously. When I write something, I have the feeling that it already exists. I depart from a general concept. I foresee more or less clearly the beginning and the end, and then I proceed to discover the intermediate pieces; but I don't have the feeling that I am inventing them; I don't feel that they depend on my judgment. I believe the same happens when we read a good poem; we believe that we could also have written that poem, that it preexisted within us. This also frequently leads us to depart from a text we've read and to compose a variation on it or a new text.

ALIFANO: I remember, Borges, that Emerson said that poetry is born from poetry.

BORGES: That is true. It is not only born from the emotion we derive

from a natural event; it can also be born from a previous poetic conception
which moves us.

ALIFANO: Yes, beauty can invade us in many ways.

BORGES: Yes, it is pursuing us everywhere. If we were sensitive enough,
we would feel it in the poetry of all languages. There's nothing strange
about so much beauty scattered about the world. My teacher, the Spanish-
Jewish poet, Rafael Cansinos-Asséns, wrote a prayer to God that said:
"Oh, Lord, let there not be so much beauty!" And I remember that
Browning wrote: "Just when we're safest, there's a sunset touch, / A fancy
from a flower-bell, someone's death, / A chorus ending from Euripides, —/
And that's enough for fifty hopes and fears/ As old and new at once as
nature's self, / To rap and knock and enter in our soul."

8

The Detective Story

> That peaceful man who uncovers
> crimes has been replaced by an
> eccentric and violent individual. . . .
> Thus, the detectives resemble the
> criminals . . .

ALIFANO: You have always been interested in the detective story, and you collaborated with Adolfo Bioy Casares in writing such stories. In addition, both of you were the founders of the series *El Séptimo Círculo* (The Seventh Circle), in which you translated and published the major works in that genre. How did you choose the title for that series?

BORGES: Bioy and I needed a title, and I suggested, "Let's see what circle violent men occupy in Dante's *Inferno*." That circle turned out to be the seventh. And it fit. If it had been the sixth, eighth or fourth it wouldn't have worked, but "The Seventh Circle" was perfect; we were lucky and we used that title for the series.

ALIFANO: Borges, let's talk about the detective story. What are its origins, as you see them?

BORGES: Several years ago I had a debate on the subject with Roger Caillois. I believe I was right and that I still am; although after a visit to Japan I've learned that one should let the other person be in the right and not oneself. At that time I was only slightly or not at all Japanese and I treated Caillois with some discourtesy and a certain harshness. I said that the detective story genre was the invention of Edgar Allan Poe, who wrote "The Murders in the Rue Morgue," "The Purloined Letter," "The Gold-Bug," and "Thou Art the Man," among other memorable stories. In those works we can find everything that was done later in the detective story. Furthermore, Poe created the fiction of the man who uncovers a crime by the use of logic, by the power of reason, and introduced the device of the story being told by a less intelligent friend—elements not found in real life, where crimes are unveiled by searches, denunciations or even mere chance,

43

but not by means of reasoning. Dupin is the sedentary man who thinks about a crime and finds the solution; and that procedure was later inherited by the famous pair of Sherlock Holmes and Watson and by Father Brown in Chesterton's stories.

ALIFANO: Is it in his short stories that Poe's main creative genius is found?

BORGES: I believe that we find in them most of his successful work, more than in any other genre he practiced, more than in his poetry and literary criticism. His detective stories earned him a place in literature. The detective novel is a genre which Poe helped to define in theory and to perfect in practice. Everything comes from him. I've always thought that Poe was aware, moreover, that the detective story falls within the genre of the fantastic. This notion is supported by the fact that he wrote in the United States, yet chose a French detective; that is, he placed him in Paris, in a remote location, which is the setting for the crimes. Undoubtedly, Poe was aware that if he had chosen New York City as the setting, his readers would have sought parallels with real life. But since he set the story in another city, he gave events a faraway and unreal quality. That is why I assert that the detective story is a genre of the fantastic.

Poe also invented the notion that something becomes invisible precisely by being too visible. In his story "The Purloined Letter," for example, Poe presents a politician who has been robbed of a very important letter. The police meticulously examine the house. They examine it with magnifying glasses; they pay close attention to the gaps between tiles, the bindings of books. They look meticulously for the hiding place, but they can't find it. Then Monsieur Auguste Dupin finds the letter: the letter is lying on top of a table! The letter was in such an obvious place, it was so open to view that for that very reason it had become invisible.

ALIFANO: That's the same idea that Chesterton uses in "The Invisible Man," isn't it?

BORGES: Ah, yes. In the tale you mention, there is a dwarf who builds mechanical servants or robots and lives in a house on a hill. All this happens in London during the winter. This gentleman receives death threats from some unknown person. Father Brown, his friend, goes out to report it to the police, and as he leaves, he asks the doorman to keep an eye on the house; he asks the same of a chestnut vendor. The murderer, of course, may enter at any moment to fulfill his threat. When Father Brown returns with the police they see footprints in the snow, footprints that go in and come out. They ask the vendor if he saw anyone entering the house; the vendor says no. They ask the doorman; the doorman also says no. Then they go up to the apartment, and there they find ashes in the chimney and the mechanical dolls. This presents the possibility that the robots had killed their creator. Then comes the solution: the crime has been committed by a character so obvious that he has become invisible. The victim had been receiving letters that were mysteriously delivered. The conclusion is this: the murderer is the mailman, who is able to enter the house unseen—unseen because he is part of the normal routine. He wears his mailman's uniform, kills his enemy, puts him in his postal bag, and burns the letters. That's the reason for the ashes in the chimney. And the footprints that come away from the house are imprinted in the snow with a greater intensity because of the weight of the corpse that the mailman carries in his bag.

ALIFANO: That plot would support your theory that the detective story is "fantastic" literature, since it raises the possibility that the mechanical dolls murdered their creator.

BORGES: Yes. And that also originates with Poe: particularly in "The Purloined Letter " and in "The Murders in the Rue Morgue." There we find the notion of a crime committed in a locked room; except that the murderer in that case turns out to be a monkey. A horrifying solution, surely, since an orangutan climbs to places that a man cannot possibly reach.

ALIFANO: Clearly then, the detective story is derived from the work of Edgar Allan Poe.

BORGES: Without a doubt. I consider Poe, as I already mentioned, its supreme creator; he is the undisputed master of the detective story. He had several reasons for devoting himself to writing such stories, besides the evident fact that his greatest ability lay in that form. During his time, if we recall a historical fact, there was a good market for such material. Magazines were full of short stories. Poe was an editor of one such magazine and he sought to please his readers by publishing quality short fiction. Most of the tales he published were written by him. When Poe began publishing his work, the short story was already flourishing in North America in the work of Irving and Hawthorne; Poe adopted the form and carried it to its utmost perfection.

ALIFANO: Can we return to your debate with Roger Caillois? What was his view on the development of the detective story?

BORGES: Well, Caillois asserted that the detective story predated Poe, since the spy or protagonist of the era of Napoleon I was, according to him, a detective story character. Now, I believe this to be a fallacy. Particularly since the mystery story has nothing to do with the detective story; it is a literary work foreign to such a genre. That there may have been spies and policemen in stories before Poe has no bearing on the matter. And, sadly, because of this debate Roger Caillois and I grew apart from one another. Later, most generously, he included a book of mine in a collection he edited and voted for me at the international Formentor Prize competition. Later we both forgot that dispute, which was obviously of no importance. But, generally, I believe that I am right, and my viewpoint that Poe was the originator of the detective story has now become the accepted view.

ALIFANO: Have other authors dealt with the origin of the detective story?

BORGES: Dorothy Sayers has criticized Edgar Allan Poe, saying that his arguments are so flimsy as to be transparent, that the reader can guess them from the very first lines. I disagree. Dorothy Sayers forgets that the reader of detective stories has been created by the very detective story genre. Thus, when one reads a detective story, one reads it with the question in mind of who is the murderer and one suspects everyone from the start. On the other hand, Poe's first readers were not readers of detective stories, so they approached their reading differently. Let's suppose, for example, that *Don Quixote* is a detective novel—fortunately, it is not; fortunately, it is something quite different. But, let's suppose that it was. Then one would read: "In a certain village in La Mancha, whose name I do not wish to recall . . . ." And one would think: "Well, the person speaking these words is, undoubtedly, the criminal, since for some reason he doesn't want to remember." And, further on, "there lived not long ago a gentleman." And one would think: "Perhaps that gentleman is alive and will be murdered, or has just been murdered." So we read a detective story suspecting everything beforehand, but the manner of reading has been created by the detective story. We, the contemporary readers of detective stories—I should exclude myself since it's been a long time since I've read any—are the children of Poe: we have been created by him. Without those first detective stories there would be neither that type of reader nor that literature. Thus, Sayers's criticism is unfounded.

ALIFANO: What is your opinion of recent authors of detective stories and novels?

BORGES: I am not really up to date on what is being written now. But based on the authors I know, I believe they have moved away from the genuine tradition of the detective short story and novel. That peaceful man who uncovers crimes has been replaced by an eccentric and violent individual. North American authors, particularly, tend to depict him with those characteristics. Thus, the detectives resemble the criminals, which, to my mind, does not fit the character of the detective story. I believe that those writers have little to do with the traditional genre created by Poe.

ALIFANO: So you disdain violence in this genre?

BORGES: Certainly. When I used to read detective stories I preferred those set in a peaceful English village. Chesterton is one of my favorite authors. All his detective stories are fantastic tales, but the fantastic quality is only suggested. As one reads on, one forgets the characteristic plot of the detective story and reads Chesterton's tales as fantastic tales. In England the detective story tradition has been more respected than in North America, where it has been replaced by novels in which violence and sex play a major part—something far removed from the literary genre invented by Poe.

ALIFANO: Let us return to Chesterton, an author you admire. Could you tell me something about him?

BORGES: With pleasure. Chesterton was a masterful writer in all the literary forms he practiced, and, as you said, I admire him greatly. He was a Christian writer, and, what's more, he was very fat. So much so that Bernard Shaw, who was fond of grand jokes, once said that the Catholic Church was a little barge in danger of sinking when Chesterton clambered on. Now Chesterton was also a great epic poet: "The Ballad of the White Horse," for example, is a remarkable poem. His metaphors are much like Victor Hugo's: they are metaphors that create a marvelous reality. As to the Father Brown stories, they almost always present a mystery that in the end has an alternative demonic or magical explanation. A novel by Chesterton that I consider remarkable is *The Man Who Was Thursday*, a book in which all the members of an anarchist society are policemen and the Police Chief is a sort of deity, implying that God is also the Devil.

ALIFANO: Which of your detective stories do you find most interesting?

BORGES: Well, one of my stories that is popular is "*El jardín de los senderos que se bifurcan*" (The Garden of Forking Paths). I also felt very proud when *Mystery Magazine*, an American publication, awarded me a prize for that story. I felt proud—and said so to my mother, who was still alive then—above all that they would take me seriously, a mere writer from the Río de la Plata.

ALIFANO: I was also expecting that you would tell me you liked the stories which you and Bioy Casares wrote under the pseudonym Bustos Domecq.

BORGES: No, I don't like those stories because of their baroque style.

But how can one write differently? I sit down to write with Bioy Casares and we are gradually transformed into that character called Bustos Domecq, or Suárez Lynch; that character takes over the action and spoils it, filling it with far-fetched events. Obviously, that third man is to be blamed for such excesses. We are but his meek though irritated scribes. But I stress, I don't like those stories at all, and, I believe, neither does Bioy.

9

Translation

I remember that Chesterton said that
he did not know Persian but that
FitzGerald's translation [of the
Rubáiyát] was too good a poem to be
faithful to the original.

ALIFANO: Almost as important as the author's work, the translator's
work allows us to know the diverse cultural traditions of the world. You
have vast experience as a translator, and on several occasions you have
referred to the subject. Shall we speak of translations and the task of translators? How should translations be done?

BORGES: At present, literal translations are in vogue. The idea of a literal
translation does not have a literary source. In my opinion, we can posit
two probable sources: one would be legal papers (the choice of legal
contracts, interpretation of documents, business agreements, etc.), which
obviously require a literal translation. (This, of course, was not the case in
past ages when there was an illustrious universal language: Latin.) The
other—doubtless more interesting—would be religious writing. An example is the Bible, a compilation of heterogenous texts from various ages
and authors, purportedly dictated to diverse scribes by the Holy Spirit.
And, according to the Kabbalists, not only the words, but also the letters
are of importance.

Obviously, then, if one attempts the translation into another language of
that sacred text, the Kabbalah, in which chance has no bearing, in which
everything has been thought out, including the letters—which, according
to the Kabbalists, have a numerical value that must be taken into account,
since a verse beginning with an A, B or C is not accidental—the
translator must seek, given the possibilities of his language, a literal
translation.

ALIFANO: What is the final result of such a procedure?

BORGES: It is appropriate, and in many cases it has resulted in phrases of admirable beauty. Hebrew, for example, has no superlatives; if I am not mistaken, in that language one cannot say "best." But a very beautiful manner of expressing it has been found: since it is impossible to say "the best night," one says "the night of nights"; since it is impossible to say "the best song," one says "The Song of Songs," which was rendered into Spanish by Fray Luis de León as "*El cantar de cantares.*"

ALIFANO: In Luther's translation of the Bible, however, to make it accessible to everyone, instead of translating "The Song of Songs," he writes "The High Song," which conveys the sense but loses the beauty of the Hebrew expression. That is misguided, isn't it?

BORGES: Yes, but in the King James Bible an effort was made to keep that beauty of diction. In it we read "A tower of strength." But Luther, who was an awful translator, renders it "A firm castle," which, as can be seen, dims the beauty of the phrase. In his translation, he also finds unacceptable "Mary, full of grace," because, he would say, it suggests the idea of a vessel. And he changes it to "Mary, you are gracious with grace." So there are cases in which the literal rendering may be beautiful, but it is not always appropriate.

ALIFANO: The same thing happens in another famous translation, one from which you often quote. I am referring to Captain Burton's translation of *The Thousand and One Nights.*

BORGES: True, Captain Burton in his version calls it *The Book of a Thousand Nights and a Night*, which is lovely in English, but I don't know how faithful to the original it may be, for if you say in Arabic "The book of the thousand nights and a night" it impresses no one. But translated into another language it sounds very good. And Burton evoked that beauty by rendering the phrase literally.

ALIFANO: Are there, however, instances in which a literal translation is questionable?

BORGES: Certainly. If in a typical novel, for example, a character says: "Buenos días!" (Good morning!), it is unacceptable to render it as "Good days!" And there are also instances in which the literal version can be beautiful, but that beauty may be an added beauty that has nothing to do with the original. Other times, there are errors. My friend Alfonso Reyes used to criticize the unforgivable error committed by Baeza, the translator of Oscar Wilde. That error destroyed the humor of Wilde's pun. Alfonso Reyes once told me, and rightly so, that *The Importance of Being Earnest* should have been translated into Spanish as *La importancia de ser Severo*. In English *earnest* means "serious" and it is also a proper name; but in Spanish *Ernesto* is merely a proper name. *Severo*, on the other hand, is closer to the sense of the title of Wilde's comedy. That title, obviously, implies a joke; the joke is lost in Baeza's translation, which turns the title into something dangling and lacking in meaning.

ALIFANO: One may conclude, then, that literal translations are less faithful to the original. How does this apply to the translation of poetry?

BORGES: Well, in the case of poetry, many translators stick to the dictionary. The dictionary is based on the hypothesis—obviously an unproven one—that languages are made up of equivalent synonyms. And it's not so. Each word has—particularly in poetry—a different affective connotation. The poem depends not only on the abstract meaning of words but also on their magical connotations. We have, for example, the case of Omar Khayyám's *The Rubáiyát*, translated by FitzGerald. This work, an excellent translation, becomes a remarkable English poem of the nineteenth century, and not a remarkable Persian poem of the eleventh century. I remember that Chesterton said that he did not know Persian but that FitzGerald's translation was too good a poem to be faithful to the original.

ALIFANO: What you're saying concurs with something Ezra Pound said about poetic translations. He said that the process of translation can help us judge a poem, since a good poem is always untranslatable. Can we infer from this notion that the translator—as some have said—must recreate the poetry or the poet's creative process?

BORGES: Undoubtedly. Furthermore, he must also be a good poet. Nowadays prose versions or literal versions are fashionable, and so from the very beginning we lose the rhythms—which to me are more essential to poetry than the abstract meaning of words, as I have mentioned. I believe that literal translations only offer help in understanding a text, but nothing more. It is now common to publish bilingual editions, which lead the translator to a more literal version, perhaps too literal, since he knows that the reader compares the original with the translation. I disagree with this editorial format, which surely works against the translator.

ALIFANO: What would be the most appropriate method for the translation of poetry?

BORGES: The method which, through close observation of the original work, finds the means of recreating what the poet said or meant. To accomplish this, a literary, not a literal, translation must be carried out. It should be noted that each language has its own possibilities and impossibilities and that these are untranslatable. For example, in Spanish we have that highly important distinction between the two verbs which mean "to be": *ser* and *estar*. SER *triste* (to be a sad person), ESTAR *triste* (to be temporarily sad); SER *enfermo* (to be a sick man), ESTAR *enfermo* (to be temporarily ill). That, as far as I know, is impossible to render in other languages.

ALIFANO: Latin, which was far superior to our present languages, had verb tenses that have been lost with the passing of time, isn't that so?

BORGES: Ah, yes. I remember a famous phrase that can exemplify your point. Roman gladiators, before entering the arena, saluted the Caesar and said: "*Salve Caesar morituri te salutam*," which translates in the best possible translation as: "Hail, Caesar, we who are about to die salute you." In Latin that was a simple expression, and that has been lost; we have lost the verb conjugation that allowed it. As I quoted that gladiators' phrase it brought to mind an anecdote of Chesterton's (perhaps somewhat beside the point, but I think worthwhile to retell). On a certain occasion he was requested to say a few words to launch a soccer match at Saint Mary's College. It is well known that Chesterton had no interest in that sport, but all the same he agreed to speak. He recalled that phrase of the gladiators and said: "Hail Mary, we who will live on salute you." A lovely variation, don't you think? Chesterton remembered the Roman gladiators and found an appropriate phrase to apply to those other gladiators who obviously didn't run the same risk as the Roman ones, who battled for their lives.

But let's consider another example of an expression in Spanish that has no equivalent in other languages. The expression, for example, "*estaba sentadita*" (she was sitting) is untranslatable into another language, because the idea of *sentadita* conveys not only the notion of someone sitting, but also creates the image of a girl who is totally vulnerable. In those words there is a tenderness that translation cannot grasp. To find an equivalent one would have to invent a similar state of being; and that can only be found by a poet. That is, the translator must also be a poet to find solutions to such problems.

ALIFANO: Are you then definitely against literal translations since you consider them alien to literature?

BORGES: Yes. And above all in poetry. Now, regarding prose, I am not sure. Perhaps it is easier, because in a novel, for example, each individual word bears less weight than in poetry, although certain words, in various instances, may be just as important. Certainly, there is no clear-cut delineation to determine whether a certain type of prose is or is not poetry. Good prose must be poetry: especially if we hold to the principle that language is born from rhythm. Thus, without excluding more abstract or didactic forms, we can say that all verbal expressions are rhythmic. How then can we distinguish between prose and poetry? That, in itself, could be a subject for another dialogue. But I conclude and insist that literal translations are foreign to literature. Of course, there are translations that are nonsensical: for example, those done by my friend Soto y Calvo, who devoted his life to translations, several of which seem more like pranks.

ALIFANO: According to Bernard Shaw, all literary work is humorous. Intentional or unintentional, this humor, he says, is found in the work of all writers.

BORGES: Ah, I didn't know that Bernard Shaw said that. In any case, I believe he is right: generally, all literary work is humorous. In John Donne's work, for example, it is somewhat intentional, conscious; in Baltasar Gracián's work it is unconscious. I was a friend of Macedonio Fernández, perhaps one of the most brilliant humorists in Argentine letters. In the style of Mark Twain, he played pranks famous throughout Buenos Aires.

ALIFANO: Was Soto y Calvo also a humorist, like Macedonio?

BORGES: No, no. Soto y Calvo was a very solemn man, almost humorless. He was a rancher, poet, translator and also an editor. As I told you, Soto y Calvo devoted all his life to translation and to poetry—an unrequited love, obviously, since he was a meager poet. Now, following Bernard Shaw's notion, I can't refer to this friend of mine except in a humorous tone. His work as a translator is full of unintentional irrelevancies, and it can't be seen in any other way except humorously.

ALIFANO: Did Soto y Calvo translate poetry also?

BORGES: Yes. And he was the only translator who translated with a knowledge of Spanish only. A curious case, isn't it?

ALIFANO: Surely.

BORGES: Soto y Calvo held to the theory that one must translate with the exact equivalence of words, in the same order and with an equal number of syllables. I pointed out to him, on a certain occasion, that this was impossible. To begin with, attempting to use the same words in the same order takes for granted that languages share similar syntax. In English, German and French one must place the subject before the verb, but this is not so in Spanish. For example, whether I say *"llegó un jinete"* or *"un jinete llegó"* it means the same: a rider arrived. But in those other languages one cannot begin a sentence with a verb. This, apparently, didn't matter at all to Soto y Calvo. He maintained that with his system one could render the correct translation.

ALIFANO: Do you remember an example of those translations?

BORGES: Yes, once he read me a translation he had done of "Al Aaraaf," that long poem by Edgar Allan Poe, where for the first time technique and poetry were fused. I remember that a verse read: "The eternal voice of God is passing by,/ And the red winds are withering in the sky." Soto y Calvo read me his translation, done with the equivalent words, in the same order and with an equal number of syllables: "*Ya no brama en la esfera del horrido aquilón*" (Has already ceased to roar in the sphere of the horrid northern wind). I, then, noted timidly that it seemed to me that they were not the same words, in the same order and with an equal number of syllables. Soto y Calvo retorted: "I expected something better from you, Borges; the eagle soars very high." This he said with a certain condescension toward me. He was, of course, the eagle.

10

North American Literature

> Mackail said that one of the gifts of
> literature is that the imaginings of one
> writer become the personal memories
> of others.

ALIFANO: Borges, in your opinion, what has been the influence of North American writers on Latin American writers?

BORGES: I believe that they have not only influenced us, but also the whole world. The literature we have created in Latin America has been important to us and, certainly, to Spain; for example, the Spanish-American literary movement *Modernismo* influenced our literature and Spain's. But what has been created in the United States has been important throughout the world. For example, we cannot think of Emerson, Walt Whitman, Edgar Allan Poe, Hawthorne, Melville, Emily Dickinson, Thoreau, Mark Twain, Henry James, without realizing that they have changed the literature of all nations.

ALIFANO: It is true. When we consider Walt Whitman, for example, we see that he changed poetry through his free verse innovation, and we realize that he is the father of all modern literature.

BORGES: Yes. Whitman, who published *Leaves of Grass* in 1855—poems obviously based on the Psalms yet distinctly different from them—is an innovator whose influence lives on even in writers who have never read him. I think that one of the great accomplishments of North Americans is their literature and the influence it has had all over the world. Let's consider three more names besides Whitman, whom you mentioned. Take Emerson. Emerson is someone to whom I personally owe a great deal. Though many would object, allow me to rank him with the others I mention here: with Melville and his wonderful nightmare of the white whale, and with Poe, that romantic who longed to be a classicist and who

55

has given us, aside from his stories, his theory of modern poetry as an intellectual exercise.

ALIFANO: Borges, this century has given us another great writer, William Faulkner, who broke away from the chronological structure of the novel. . . .

BORGES: Ah, but of course Faulkner, who represents the southern United States and who attempted so many felicitous experiments, among them the one you noted: his departure from chronology and his practice of merging different planes of time. I will mention another name: Robert Frost, that great poet whose work is a mirror of man's essential loneliness.

ALIFANO: What a magnificent poet! I remember those lines from "Birches": "I'd like to get away from the earth awhile/ And then come back to it and begin over." Do you remember them?

BORGES: Yes. In that poem Frost imagines that a child climbs a tree, a birch tree, and that he sways at the top of it until the branch bends down to the earth. In that poem Frost reveals man's desire to ascend to heaven and to return again to earth. I often think of two religious poems by Frost, "A Masque of Reason" and "Once in the Pacific," and that other poem, entitled "The Bear," which says: "Man acts more like the poor bear in a cage."

ALIFANO: Faulkner's influence on all Latin American writers is very marked, isn't it, Borges?

BORGES: Yes. Particularly in Cortázar, don't you agree? Well, one can say so much about Faulkner. . . . For him the human mind and human nature is a terrifying thing; it is a depthless abyss that fascinates him and into which he constantly delves. One of his favorite themes is the decadence and fall of southern families. He was a southerner, gripped by a tradition which he did not accept and which he never stopped fighting. I think that he, better than any other writer, expresses that conflict from which southerners, most likely, still suffer.

ALIFANO: Yes, there is a sort of bond of love and hate which, as you've said, links Faulkner to the southern tradition. And this is manifest in almost all his novels, isn't that so?

BORGES: I think that it is particularly clear in *The Sound and the Fury*, the Faulkner novel that I remember best. It treats the theme of members— well, let's say degenerates—of a southern family. A mother who is incapable of raising and educating her children; a father demented by alcoholism; a daughter who commits incest with her brother and bears an illegitimate daughter who, as an adult, elopes with a comedian; another son who is a killer; another who I believe is mentally retarded; and there is a third one who enters Harvard but then commits suicide. That entire story presents the human mind as something terrifying. The soul's worth is presented through frustration, and essentially it is a tale that depicts moral bankruptcy. In that novel, the blacks, the black servants, the idiot and an uncle, also a mentally retarded man, are the only characters who awaken some sympathy in the reader.

ALIFANO: The literary legacy of Melville is also important, don't you think so, Borges?

BORGES: Ah, but of course. But Melville's influence is less direct. How odd! And this is also true in all of English-speaking literature: Melville's tradition had become almost extinct at the beginning of the twentieth century; later, toward the end of the 1920s, it had a revival. Hawthorne experienced a similar fate. Here is an intriguing fact about Melville: if you compare the canto on Ulysses in *The Divine Comedy* and the last chapter of *Moby Dick*, you will see that they are alike. Obviously, the words differ, but the events are the same. The ship sinks with its entire crew, the sea engulfs them, there is despair.... Dante certainly expresses it in a more emphatic and laconic manner, but surely the event is the same.

ALIFANO: Melville must have been aware of that.

BORGES: I would think so. Melville could not have been ignorant of it, since his friend Longfellow had introduced him to *The Divine Comedy*. It is well known that Melville was considerably influenced by Hawthorne. *The Scarlet Letter* fascinated Melville, who admitted being bewitched by his compatriot's novel. Upon discovering Hawthorne, Melville said that he had finally found a man to keep him company in the midst of his solitude. Later, they became personal friends.

ALIFANO: How difficult to imagine such a close relationship between the intense and impulsive Herman Melville and the restrained and somber Nathaniel Hawthorne! Don't you think so?

BORGES: True. They were two seemingly opposite spirits. But I believe they got along well and were good friends. *Moby Dick*, in a sense, is a fortunate consequence of that friendship. Also, Melville wrote a poem entitled "Monody" on Hawthorne's death.

ALIFANO: Mark Twain is another literary genius that I would like us to discuss.

BORGES: Certainly he was a man of genius. I have noted an odd fact regarding Mark Twain, a sort of genealogy: in the 1880s *The Adventures of Huckleberry Finn* appeared. In broad outline it is the description of a state, a country, a region as seen through the eyes of a child and an adult, a black fugitive. This book was read and reread by Kipling, who in 1901 published that wonderful novel *Kim*. And in it we find a description of India—a country which certainly doesn't look like the southern United States before the Civil War—as seen by a child and a lama, who is an old man. The theme is also the friendship between the two of them. And then we have another book written by the Argentine Ricardo Güiraldes, a reader of Kipling. *Don Segundo Sombra*, as that novel is entitled, has a similar outline to the other two, except that in this novel the events take place in the province of Buenos Aires. The characters, however, are a child and an old man. Thus, these novels are essentially related. In all three a region and an era are described as seen by a child and an adult.

ALIFANO: Undoubtedly there is a genealogy: each book was inspired by the previous book, which illustrates that literature is a living thing that branches out. It confirms Emerson's belief that poetry is born from poetry.

BORGES: True. It seems a healthy thing that that should have happened. The three novelists were great writers who created, each in turn, three famous books. Mackail said that one of the gifts of literature is that the imaginings of one writer become the personal memories of others. For example, in thinking of *Huckleberry Finn*, I don't think of the book with a red cover that is here in my library, a short distance from where we are sitting; rather I think of the Mississippi, which I have barely glanced at, and of the nights on a raft that form no part of my destiny, but certainly do shape the destiny of that child imagined or dreamed by Mark Twain.

ALIFANO: Mark Twain had a positive influence on the Argentine novelist Macedonio Fernández; his humor was similar to Twain's.

BORGES: Yes. Macedonio was a devotee of Mark Twain. I remember that he was once asked what he thought of Góngora, and he answered: "I don't sleep facing that side; Quevedo and Twain keep me awake." Oddly, Twain was born the year Halley's comet appeared, I think it was in 1835. And he said that he would die the year that Halley's comet reappeared. In 1910 Halley's comet reappeared, and that year Mark Twain died.

ALIFANO: Mark Twain led a life almost as adventuresome as the one he invented in his fiction.

BORGES: Well, few people know that he fought in the Civil War for fifteen days as a volunteer—for the South, of course. Later the group that Mark Twain was with killed a man, and they were so shocked that they disbanded. Mark Twain was also a riverboat pilot on the Mississippi, and a goldminer in California, like Stevenson, another writer who greatly admired him. Kipling wanted to know Twain personally, and he traveled to the United States to meet him. That meeting impressed him greatly, and he always remembered it. In a book entitled *From Sea to Sea* Kipling described in detail his visit with Twain, but he regretted that he was unable to meet Stevenson.

ALIFANO: Regrettably, Twain, unlike Faulkner, for example, has not influenced other Latin American writers.

BORGES: No, he has not, but no doubt that is because of a deficiency in us. We have not been worthy, as Macedonio Fernández was, of a writer of genius such as Mark Twain.

11

Time

ALIFANO: But why is time ungraspable?
BORGES: Undoubtedly, because time is made up of memory. . . . And that memory is made up largely of forgetfulness.

ALIFANO: Time is undoubtedly an essential theme—one you have treated often in your work. Shall we talk about it?

BORGES: I remember that Nietzsche, who was reckless and absolutist in his opinions, was angered when Goethe and Schiller were spoken of in the same breath. It seems to me that we could apply the same notion when referring to time and to space. It is equally irreverent to speak of time and space, placing them both on the same level, for we can dismiss space from our thinking, but no matter what, we cannot cast off time. Let's suppose that the visual world—our visual world—disappears because we possess one sense, rather than five. That one sense could be hearing; that is, we have only ears. All our surroundings vanish; the stars disappear, the landscape, the sky. If we are deprived of touch, the texture of materials, the smooth, the rough surfaces disappear . . . and if we lose our sense of taste and our sense of smell we also lose all those sensations experienced in the mouth and the nose.

ALIFANO: We would then have a world which could do without space?

BORGES: Yes. We would have a world of individuals who could communicate only by means of words, and, of course, also through music. That is to say, we would have a world in which there would be nothing save consciousness and music. Well, one could object to this—someone could justifiably object that there could be no music without instruments. But I believe that it is nonsense to suppose that music requires instruments. It is true that instruments are needed for the production of music; but if we think of such and such a score, we can imagine it without instruments, without violins, pianos, organs. As Schopenhauer noted, music is not something that is added to the world: music is a world in itself.

ALIFANO: But let's return to time. That imaginary world made up of nothing but consciousness and music—undoubtedly as complex as the world in which we live—could it cast off time?

BORGES: No. There's no way we can imagine it without time. Because time is the essential problem of existence. Time is succession. To exist is to *be* time. We are time; I mean that we cannot cast off time. Our consciousness is continuously passing from one state to another, and that is time, succession.

ALIFANO: Henri Bergson said somewhere that time is the central problem of metaphysics.

BORGES: And it is so. If that problem had been solved, everything else, obviously, would have been solved. I am not so sure, for example, that after twenty or thirty years of study and meditation, which has been the cause of so many sleepless nights for philosophers, we've made any progress on the essential problem of time. I would assert that we always feel that strange perplexity which Heraclitus poignantly expressed in his dictum: "One cannot step twice into the same river." First of all because the waters of a river flow, are never still. And secondly—this is something that concerns us metaphysically, that produces in us a sort of sacred horror—because we ourselves are a river, a river that continuously flows, we also are ever-changing.

ALIFANO: Quevedo defined time as an enemy that kills as it flees. But why is time ungraspable?

BORGES: Undoubtedly, because time is made up of memory. We are each, to a great extent, made up of our poor and frail memory. And that memory is made up largely of forgetfulness. That magnificent line of Boileau once again comes to mind: "Time flies and draws us with it. The moment in which I am speaking is already far from me." That is to say, my present, or whatever my present was, is already the past.

ALIFANO: But have solutions been found? More precisely, have there been attempts to solve that puzzle that time presents to us?

BORGES: Certainly. The oldest that I can remember is that of Plato, which then Plotinus attempts to confront, and later Saint Augustine. Plato tried to solve the problem of time by creating one of the most beautiful concepts of mankind: eternity. I am not a believer, that is why I refer to eternity as an invention. Religious thinkers would define in another way that which I call a human invention. But that is another question altogether, one we can leave for a future conversation.

ALIFANO: What is, in your opinion, eternity? How would you define it?

BORGES: I believe that eternity is the summation of all yesterdays. Eternity is all of our yesterdays, all the yesterdays of all conscious human beings. Eternity is the past, that past unknown to us; I believe we will never know when it began. But eternity is also the whole present. It is this moment which envelops us all; all the cities of the world, all the worlds, all space. And, in addition, eternity is the future. That future as yet uncreated, but which exists, which at this very moment is beginning to exist.

ALIFANO: Do you mean then, that, from a theological perspective, eternity is an instant in which, miraculously, those various times converge?

BORGES: Yes. And to give greater breadth to that concept, we could refer to the first solution—Plato's. This solution can seem arbitrary; I believe, however, that it is not, and I hope to find a way to demonstrate it. Plato said that time is the moving image of eternity. Consider: Plato begins from eternity, from an eternal being. That eternal being longs to project itself in other beings, and it cannot do so enclosed in its eternity; it has to do it in succession. That is why Plato says that time is the moving image of eternity.

ALIFANO: Remember the definition of Plotinus, someone who felt so acutely the problem of time?

BORGES: I remember it well. Plotinus says that there are three times, and the three times are in the present. One is the now, the moment in which I speak. That is to say, the moment in which I spoke, because already that moment belongs to the past. And then we have another moment, which is the past in the present; that which we call memory. And then another, the future in the present, which is that which our hope or fear imagines.

ALIFANO: There's also a fundamental statement by the English mystic William Blake, closely related to those concepts you've just mentioned.

BORGES: Ah, yes! William Blake says: "Time is the gift of eternity." Let's try to expand on those truly wise words: if all Being were revealed to us—the Being rather than the world—at a single instant, undoubtedly we would be annihilated, killed. Thus, as Blake says, "time is the gift of eternity"; that is to say, eternity allows us all those experiences in succession. Thus, we have days and nights, hours and years. We have memory, we have our present perceptions, and then we have the future whose shape we are ignorant of, but which we foresee or fear. All, absolutely all, is given to us sequentially, and wisely so, I should add, for if it were given to us all of a sudden, it would be impossible for human beings to endure such a terrible vision—the unbearable burden of the whole Being of the universe.

I remember that Schopenhauer, whom I already quoted, said that, fortunately for us, our life is divided into days and nights, our life is broken up by sleep. Thus we get up every morning, we live through our day, then we sleep. If there were no sleep, living would be unbearable, and we would not be able to contain pleasure; perhaps there would be no pleasure. The totality of Being is unattainable to us. All is given us, but, thankfully, gradually.

ALIFANO: We mentioned Plotinus, Plato, Boileau and Blake, but I believe we've omitted someone who felt the problem of time with extraordinary depth; I am referring to Saint Augustine. Perhaps one of the most anguished thinkers in his attempt to solve time's riddle.

BORGES: Yes. I believe that no one has felt time with such intensity as Saint Augustine. He says his soul burns, that it is burning because it longs to know what time is, and he asks God to reveal it to him. Not because of vain curiosity, but because he can't go on living not knowing what time is. *That* is the essential question for Saint Augustine. Bergson would later refer to this as the fundamental problem of metaphysics. And I would add that time is not only the supreme question of metaphysics but our main and only problem, for we are time. Who is each one of us? Who am I? Perhaps we'll never know. Meanwhile, as Saint Augustine said, we burn to know it.

12

The Kabbalah

How does "The Song of Songs" differ
from a poem? It leads us to suppose
that sacred texts have infinite meaning.

ALIFANO: Borges, there's a subject which is undeniably linked to the
word and which has always interested you. I am referring to the Kabbalah.
Where does the name come from?

BORGES: The diverse doctrines that shaped the Kabbalah come from a
concept that, in my opinion, is quite foreign to our Western culture. This
concept is based on the idea of a sacred book. In the Western world we
sustain a belief that attempts to approximate that concept, but which, in
my opinion, is mistaken; I am referring to the classic book. Let us consider
it. The word *classic* finds its etymology in the Latin word *classis,* which
means a frigate, a fleet. A classic book is a book which is as orderly as
things on board a ship are. That is to say, a classic work must be, essentially, an eminent book within its genre. *The Divine Comedy, Don Quixote,*
Faust, The Iliad, to name a few, are classic works. Now, in literary history
there are no known absolute texts; human texts are imperfect. The notion
of the sacred book is entirely different from the notion of a classic book.
A sacred book is an absolute book, a perfect book, a book dictated by an
infinite intelligence which has condescended to permit human beings to
write it down.

ALIFANO: In other words, a book written by God?

BORGES: Yes. This idea, as Spengler points out and proves in *Der*
Untergang des Abendlandes (The Decline of the West), occurs in all
religions. But going back to what I said initially: The Greeks, for example,
never believed that *The Iliad* was a perfect book. They considered it an
eminent book, it was seen as the epitome, as the height of poetry, but they
did not believe that each word, each hexameter, was inevitably admirable.

I now remember a phrase of Horace which applies to this case and will lead us back to the theme of the Kabbalah; Horace said: "Sometimes our good Homer falls asleep; the good Holy Spirit never does." The *modus operandi* of the Kabbalists is based on a logical premise, on the idea that a sacred book is an absolute text in which nothing is a result of chance. That is, it is a text dictated by an infinite intelligence.

ALIFANO: In that case the word would be the primary source and testimony. Isn't that so?

BORGES: Certainly. Words were the instruments of God's work. The Spanish writer Saavedra Fajardo also agrees with this. God creates the world by means of words; that is, God said, "Let there be light" and there was light. From that, one concludes that the world was created by the word "light." If God had said another word and with a different intonation, it would have resulted, obviously, not in light but something else.

ALIFANO: What is the precise meaning of the word "Kabbalah," Borges?

BORGES: The word "Kabbalah" comes from the Hebrew and means "tradition." This word denotes an interpretative system of the Holy Scriptures, a Jewish system of exegesis that leads to an approach to God and to the understanding of the universe.

ALIFANO: The first Kabbalists appeared in Spain, during the Talmudic era, isn't that so, Borges?

BORGES: Yes, in the twelfth and thirteenth centuries. Its precise place of origin is Catalonia; later it spread to France, Italy and Germany, and to some degree everywhere else.

ALIFANO: Well, we have already established the difference between a classic book and a sacred book, and the origin of the Kabbalah. Can we now speak about the method of the Kabbalists?

BORGES: Well, when the Kabbalists study they attempt, I suspect, to incorporate Gnostic thought into Jewish mysticism, so as to justify it as a sacred text, to make it orthodox. I don't think that the Kabbalists dedicated themselves to this study for mere pleasure or for the religious consolation that man can find in the company of his God. It seems to me that they did it with the intention of returning to the first moment of Creation. And as the Torah, indifferent to the contingencies of time, narrates the Genesis, the initial creative process, it is sufficient to examine it to find the path back to the realm where God rules. That text of an infinite intelligence, dictated by the Holy Spirit, leads the Kabbalists to read it in every possible way—from right to left, from left to right, and so on—and then leads them to reinterpret some letters in relation to others, also to seek the symbolic meaning of the words.

ALIFANO: So that in analyzing those texts, it is as though they are analyzing something as amazing as the very mystery of Creation?

BORGES: True. And that clashes somewhat with our Western thinking. As I said, when we think of words, we think, from an historical perspective, that the words were initially sounds, and that later they were divided into letters. In the Kabbalah, on the other hand, it is supposed that letters antedated the words; that is, that the letters, not the words denoted by the letters, were the instruments of God. It would be like believing that the Letter, as every experience, came before the diction of the words, and so there is no element of causality in the sacred texts; everything is pre-ordained, including, for example, the number of letters. Later, relations between letters were invented.

ALIFANO: Consequently, the Kabbalists study the sacred text as though it were coded, isn't that so?

BORGES: Yes. It is studied as if it were cryptography, is interpreted as such, and various laws are invented to decipher it. For example: one can take each letter of the sacred text and see what other words begin with that letter, and then read those words and proceed in this manner for each letter of the text.

ALIFANO: Did this coded writing, this cryptography, lead the Kabbalists to logical conclusions?

BORGES: Certainly. Its point of departure is the notion that God's intelligence is infinite; consequently, this cryptography can be deciphered, and its results are worthy of consideration, since God himself has preordained those results. By means of studying that coded writing, by means of that toil, which resembles the labor in "The Gold-Bug," by Edgar Allan Poe, one arrives at the Doctrine.

ALIFANO: It is fitting to ask, Borges: does the Doctrine precede the method of the Kabbalists?

BORGES: I suspect that it does. I suspect that what happened with the Kabbalah is similar to what occurred with Spinoza's philosophy: its logical structure came after it. I think that the Kabbalists must have been influenced by the Gnostics of Alexandria and that their doctrine could very well have derived from them. Then, so that all of it would fit with Hebrew tradition, the Kabbalists sought that odd method of deciphering the letters.

ALIFANO: Could you give an example of that method applied to the study of the Bible?

BORGES: Well, I would do it by referring to *Don Quixote*, a book we all know. That novel begins with two monosyllabic words ending in *n*: *en un* (in a), which are followed by a five-letter word, *lugar* (place), then by two two-letter words, *de la* (of the), and then by *Mancha*, which can be considered a five- or six-letter word depending on whether we consider *ch* as two letters or as a single one. If someone pretended to derive logical conclusions from this, we would think he was insane or that he was going insane. The Bible, however, has been studied in that manner by the Kabbalists. They say, for example, that it begins with the letter *beth*, the first letter of *Bereshith*. Why does it state, for example, "In the beginning, gods creates the heavens and the earth" using a plural subject and the verb in the singular? Why does it begin with *B*? That first letter in Hebrew most likely corresponds to the initial letter of the Spanish word *bendición* (blessing). The text could not begin with a letter that corresponds to a curse; it had to begin with a blessing: *beth* is the first Hebrew letter of *baruch*, which means "blessing."

ALIFANO: Borges, is that curious method of the Kabbalists based on some premise, some essential concept?

BORGES: It is based on one which, in my opinion, is fundamental: the idea that sacred writings are absolute texts, and that in a sacred text nothing results from chance. But let's return to the example of *Don Quixote*. Let us suppose that Cervantes was the Holy Spirit (fortunately, he was not, and his work belongs to admirable human texts, imperfect but brilliant creations); then the fact that his book begins with *En*, a monosyllabic word ending in *n*, and that it goes on to another, *un*, also ending in *n*, and then to *lugar* (place), a five-letter word, and then to *de la* (of the) would not have been accidental, because nothing can be accidental in an absolute text. But, as I said, there are no absolute texts; in any case, human texts are not. However, in a text composed by the Holy Spirit, by an infinite intelligence, why should we assume it has any cracks? Why should we suppose any vacillation? Why should we suppose any weakness? It must be completely inevitable. And from that inevitability, the Kabbalists—by the process of reinterpreting letters, by substituting one letter with others and by searching for their symbolism—deduced that system known as the Kabbalah. A system which seems to me justified, for if the Sacred Book is not an infinite text, then how would it differ from so many human books? How does "The Song of Songs" differ from a poem? It leads us to suppose that sacred texts have infinite meaning. Johannes Scotus Erigena, in a famous statement, illustrated this better than anyone when he likened the Bible and its infinite meaning to the iridescent plumage of the peacock.

13

The Tango

The tango, which already had an
international passport and had been
much cleaned up in Paris, still was not
liked by decent people who knew that
it came from the brothel and that it
was sexual and aggressive.

ALIFANO: Borges, I know you like the *milonga* more than the tango.
Could you tell me why?

BORGES: Well, it's because I am bothered by the sentimentality of the
tango, which goes from defiance and courage to a sentimental and whining
tone. There is a misconception about the tango: it is not the native music of
the barrios of Buenos Aires but rather of its brothels. I have always maintained that our characteristic music is the *milonga*. The *milonga* is an
infinite celebration which narrates, in a restrained manner, duels and
bloody deeds, deaths and provocations; never strident, it is a mixture of
dialogue and serenity. I think that the *milonga* is one of the great means of
conversation in Buenos Aires, much like the *truco*, that card game filled
with dialogue and mischief.

ALIFANO: And yet the tango is an element of Buenos Aires, and like
every reality, it holds a secret. I propose that we inquire into it: in your
opinion, what is the origin of the tango?

BORGES: I have always concurred with the conclusion of three of its
researchers who, in various ways and from diverse perspectives, have
traced its history. I am referring to Muzzio Saenz Peña, Vicente Rossi and
Carlos Vega. All three reach the same conclusion: the tango originated in
the brothels. There is a widely held view, however—frequently promoted
in the movies and the theater—that the tango was born in the shantytowns
of La Boca del Riachuelo. The picturesque features of the place and its
photographic attractions have led enthusiasts of that music (for the most

part not very profound devotees) to concur with that viewpoint.

ALIFANO: I now remember that in your book *Evaristo Carriego* you showed your preference for the former origin, and you added that you had carried out certain research that confirmed it.

BORGES: Yes. I did that research with the assistance of my friends. My friendship with the *guapo* Nicolás Paredes, for example, allowed me to become acquainted personally with don José Saborido, the composer of the tango "*La morocha*" (The Dark-Skinned Girl); I also talked with Ernesto Poncio, the composer of "*Don Juan*," and later with the brothers of Vicente Greco, who composed "*La viruta*" (The Wood Shavings) and "*La tablada*" (Destined for the Slaughterhouse), two very famous tangos of that era.

ALIFANO: Did those individuals agree in their opinions, Borges?

BORGES: Generally they did, although with some variations. Concerning the essential elements, which I was interested in, I think that they all agreed; they asserted that the tango definitely originated in the brothels. I remember that Saborido, who was Uruguayan, held that it began in Montevideo; Ernesto Poncio opted for his barrio and for the brothels operating in the street fairs of the Retiro suburb. A few years later, when I was working for the newspaper *Crítica* I researched this subject once again, and I remember that the *porteños* (residents of Buenos Aires) of the southern barrios supported the view that the tango began in Chile Street; on the other hand, the *porteños* of the northern barrios held that it had begun in Temple Street, that red light district which now is called Viamonte and runs through the very heart of Buenos Aires. Some of them also mentioned the brothels of Junín Street, around the *Once* barrio. But all, without exception, concurred that the tango began in the brothels.

ALIFANO: Are the precise dates when the tango began known, Borges?

BORGES: I remember that Muzzio Saenz Peña, who researched that question, concluded that probably the tango started to be played in Buenos Aires in the 1880s; so the tango was born sometime between 1880 and 1890.

ALIFANO: There must have been a unanimous rejection of that music from the outlying neighborhoods.

BORGES: There was. The wealthy class, high society, above all, did not want anything to do with that music from the whorehouses. But by 1910, most likely indoctrinated by the good example of Paris, the same people had relented and opened their doors to the tango, that great personage who returned triumphantly from Europe, although he had been born in the brothels of Buenos Aires.

ALIFANO: What instruments did those early tango musicians play, Borges?

BORGES: It is said that the original instruments used by the orchestras were the violin, the flute and the piano; later, I believe much later, the concertina was added. This in a certain way proves my theory—more precisely the theory held by others and that I accept—that the tango was not born in the shantytowns in the outskirts of the city. In those districts the usual instrument was the guitar, played by singers who came from the countryside. But there are other facts that confirm this theory: women did not want to participate in these dances of whores. I am referring, of course, to the women of the lower classes, for they saw in this music something vile and disgraceful. Those who indulged in it were tainted with lasciviousness, and it is better not to remember the titles of those tangos: "*El fierrazo*" (The Iron Bar), "*La parda*" (The Mulatto Woman), "*El choclo*" (The Corncob). I remember that when I was a child in Palermo, my neighborhood, I used to see men dancing with each other on the streetcorners; the dance, of course, was the tango. Those images were splendidly captured by Evaristo Carriego in his *Misas herejes* (Heresy Masses), when he says in memorable poetry: "*En la calle, la buena gente derrocha/ Sus guarangos decires más lisonjeros,/ Porque al compás de un tango, que es La morocha,/ Lucen ágiles cortes dos orilleros.*" (In the street, the bystanders squander/ Gross and flattering sayings,/ For following the waves of that tango, "*La morocha*"/ Two men dazzle with their steps.)

ALIFANO: Now tell me, Borges, how did the tango win over the common man? How has it come to be the most popular and typical music of Buenos Aires?

BORGES: Well, that "reptile of the brothel," as Leopoldo Lugones defines it with a certain spiteful tone in his book *El payador* (The Itinerant Singer), had to struggle hard to triumph at the downtown dancing halls; even in the outskirts it was not easy. The tango, which already had an international passport and had been much cleaned up in Paris, still was not liked by decent people who knew that it came from the brothel and that it was sexual and aggressive.

ALIFANO: Let us talk a little about that characteristic pugnaciousness of the tango in which you have shown so much interest.

BORGES: Yes. I have noted the similarities and relations that this pugnacious character of the tango has with certain types of literary writing. The tango expresses directly something that poets of different ages have tried to put into words: the conviction that to fight can be a sort of fiesta.

It reminds me that in *The Iliad*, for example, the Achaens considered war sweeter than the return to their beloved native land; we also know the attitude of Paris, Priam's son, who ran swiftly and joyously to engage in the brutal battle.

ALIFANO: Does that harsh and quarrelsome tone that you attribute to the tango have a sexual as well as a bellicose origin?

BORGES: I believe that those currents have a similar impulse. The word *man*, for example, connotes a bellicose and sexual capacity in all the languages I know. The Latin word *virtus*, for instance, means courage: that Latin word comes from *vir*, which means *male*. In the tango both elements are found. The first composers generally sought malevolent and sexual qualities. But they did not scorn the elements of joy, humor and color, although they always kept their songs full of boasts and challenges. Those composers closely resemble the itinerant singers, the *payadores*, who came before them, and in a certain way, they also resemble the precursors of the *payadores*. The tango, especially the old tango, the so-called *tango-milonga*, is music that usually conveys that bellicose joy whose verbal expression was attempted in another century by the Greek and Germanic rhapsodists. Now, the authors of the lyrics of tangos have always sought that courageous tone, that brusque and friendly tone, and they have written some quite successful works which we can certainly place within that tradition.

ALIFANO: At first the tango had no lyrics, isn't that so?

BORGES: Yes, in the beginning it didn't, but as soon as lyrics were added to it, those lyrics were occasional and obscene; almost always full of boasts. I remember these verses from a *tango-milonga*: "Soy del barrio del *Alto,/ Soy del barrio del Retiro./ Yo soy aquél que no miro/ Con quién tengo que pelear,/ Y a quien en el milonguear,/ Ninguno se puso a tiro.*" (I am from the barrio del Alto,/ From the barrio del Retiro./ I am one who never worries/ What guy I am going to fight,/ And I remain unequaled/ in the art of dancing the *milonga*.)

ALIFANO: What delightful lines! It is a shame that the tango turned into nostalgic music, particularly the sung tango, don't you think?

BORGES: Yes, it ends up acquiring a sentimental tone; undoubtedly, the nostalgic tone of the European immigrant. From then on it becomes the poetical theme of the suburbs. The anguish of clandestine love affairs flowed through the pen of popular authors, and, well, the tango becomes mocking, rancorous, recriminating toward the unfaithful woman. It becomes, then, a tango of misery and lament. All the hustle and bustle of the city, all the emotions that move men—anger, fear, desire, sexual pleasure—become central motifs for the authors of tangos. I don't think it is absurd to consider the tango as a vast expression of the incoherent *comédie humaine* of the life of Buenos Aires.

14

Arturo Capdevilla

He spoke in a very Spanish manner.
It is said that in Spain he would speak
in this way with such devotion that
not even the Spaniards themselves
understood him.

ALIFANO: Borges, which literary merits or qualities do you consider to be most important in the work of the Argentine poet Arturo Capdevilla?

BORGES: I think that his work has many literary qualities that have been only slightly emphasized. A few days ago Adolfo Bioy Casares noted that if one were to judge Arturo Capdevilla based on his best poems, one would see that he is clearly superior to Leopoldo Lugones. Lugones, perhaps, doesn't have a poem comparable to such poems by Capdevilla as "*Aulo Gelio*" (Aulus Gellius) or "*La Fiesta del mundo*" (The Feast of the World). This is because in Lugones's work beauty and ugliness coexist, a quality also found in Quevedo. I remember, for example, that famous sonnet by Lugones entitled: "*Oceánida*" (Oceanid), which has two lovely lines that read: "*Esa luz de tardes mortecinas/ que en el agua pacífica perdura.*" (That light of dying afternoons/ That in peaceful waters lives on). But that very same sonnet begins with these somewhat inexplicable and unpleasant lines: "*El mar lleno de urgencias masculinas/ bramaba alrededor de tu cintura*" (The sea, full of masculine desires,/ Roared about your waist). And then the poem ends with these two lines, which seem to me even worse: "*Y al penetrar entre tus muslos finos/ la onda se aguzó como una daga*" (And as it dug between your fine thighs/ The wave narrowed like a dagger). It would be better not to remember those lines. Similarly, those other lines from the sonnet "*Delectación Morosa*" (Morose Delight), which read: "*Poblóse de murciélagos el combo/ cielo, a manera de chinesco biombo*" (Bats invaded the convex/ sky resembling a Chinese screen). And yet, that

75

same sonnet ends with those admirable lines: "*Y a nuestros pies un río de jacinto/ corría sin rumor hacia la muerte*" (And at our feet a river of hyacinths/ Ran without a sound toward our death). But, well, you proposed to speak about Capdevilla, so let us stop criticizing Lugones.

ALIFANO: Yes, Borges, but you began with an interesting comparison between the two authors.

BORGES: Ah, yes. Well, I would say that if in his best creations Capdevilla is better than Lugones, it is because he doesn't write in a self-important style. Capdevilla was a man who was indifferent to fashionable styles or innovations. That attitude, which is not in the least egotistical, is paid for with neglect. I tell you, I am possibly repeating myself (for I believe that we have talked about this previously), that the aspect I deplore in the baroque style is that it is an egotistical style.

ALIFANO: Pardon me, Borges, but if you hold that view, you are condemning the baroque style not only because of esthetic but also ethical considerations.

BORGES: True. Notice that when a writer becomes accustomed to the baroque style, he attempts to surprise the reader with every line he writes, and that becomes a fault. I don't know whether that can be attributed to vanity, but certainly to impertinence. It is bothersome for the reader to be continuously surprised. On the other hand, what we term the classical style has the advantage that it doesn't seek to surprise us with each line, that it seeks rather to persuade us, to project an emotion without calling too much attention to the means. Now, I wonder: why is Capdevilla an almost forgotten poet? In Spain, for example, when I mentioned his name, no one had heard of him; he, who had loved Spain so dearly. And here, in Argentina, well, I would say that he is also a forgotten poet.

ALIFANO: You've said that Capdevilla was indifferent to poetic fashions. If we add to that the fact that, similar to Enrique Banchs, he did not create a literary movement, it would further explain why he has been forgotten.

BORGES: It's true. That is the reason. We tend to judge poetry and literature by their relationship to literary history. In France, for example, writers write on the basis of literary history. A poet begins by defining his purposes and then writes his work. That doesn't happen in England, which is a country of individuals. In France, however, which is also a country made up of individualistic people (there is no one more individualistic than Hugo or Verlaine), writers, nevertheless, begin to write conscious of their place in literary history. That is why France abounds in polemics, manifestos, and literary movements. In England this doesn't happen. I think that a concern with literary movements can explain our unjust neglect of Capdevilla.

Let's suppose, for example, that Capdevilla or Enrique Banchs never existed. Well, as for Banchs, I believe our loss would be his book *La urna* (The Urn), and some sonnets that he wrote later; we can without any risk forget *Las barcas* (The Ships), *El cascabel del halcón* (The Falcon's Rattle) and *El libro de los elogios* (The Book of Praise). Now, suppose that we lose the work of Arturo Capdevilla. In that case, we lose admirable books. But literary history, nevertheless, remains unchanged, since he did not have any followers.

We tend to suppose that a poet is good when he is a forerunner. Let's take a well-known case, that of Bartolomé Hidalgo, the originator of *gaucho* poetry. If Hidalgo had not inspired Ascasubi or Estanislao del Campo and Hernández, we would have forgotten him. So we always tend to judge a work in relation to literary history. Capdevilla was a very well-educated man who wrote in a style—I wouldn't say anonymous, for in every writer there is always something personal—but which, first of all, did not have followers and, moreover, was not innovative. In the case of Banchs something similar happened. Both were admirable poets who were not innovative, and that had a price, as we see. On the other hand, a greater importance is given to a minor poet who has originated a style or, in the case of Hidalgo, was the first to have the notion to present a dialogue between two gauchos and have them speak a studied rural and rustic language. Capdevilla has left us nothing more and nothing less than remarkable poems.

ALIFANO: Don't you think that another element that has contributed to our neglect of Capdevilla is the fact that his work is very diverse? Capdevilla touched on many themes.

BORGES: Ah, of course: that's also true. But the same could be said of Shakespeare. That happens with any prolific writer who has some books that are more admirable than others or even some that are not in the least admirable. Capdevilla had a great curiosity. He wrote on such diverse themes as *The Thousand and One Nights* and medicine, and one could perhaps condemn that. In writing about *The Thousand and One Nights*, he used the least faithful translation of that work. Capdevilla worked from a translation by Mardrus, and together with Cancela he praised it highly. That French translation is obviously apocryphal; it is done in a modernist style and is full of art nouveau landscapes. If one compares it to other translations, even with Burton's, its exaggeration of the original text becomes obvious. Since what he read was a stimulus for things he would do later, I don't think that one should use that as an argument against Capdevilla. In the end, it doesn't matter that he worked from a version of *The Thousand and One Nights* now judged to be faulty. That was simply his point of departure.

ALIFANO: And what about the texts that Arturo Capdevilla wrote about medicine?

BORGES: Capdevilla was one year from graduating as a physician. He began writing on medicine by imagining a Greek physician and attributing his own theories to him. It was somewhat similar to Carlyle's procedure in his exposition on idealism, which he attributed to an imaginary German philosopher. Capdevilla began writing comments on that imaginary Greek physician, and then he ventured fully into the theme and wrote books on medicine. Those books were based on his own research, which was also quite coherent.

ALIFANO: How did people receive this poet's venture into medicine?

BORGES: Not very well. People said to themselves before reading those works, "Capdevilla is a poet. Why does he have to stick his nose into medicine?" That prejudice, I think, is illogical. The fact that an observation or development of a scientific theory was carried out by a poet does not mean that it is necessarily erroneous. Capdevilla, for example, had his own theory concerning leprosy. He observed that leprosy occurs in riverside areas; he asserted that in Argentina it began in El Tigre, in the lower Belgrano district, and that it then extended throughout all the islands south of the province of Buenos Aires. Capdevilla attributed the occurrence of leprosy to the diet of the people, which consisted mainly of fish and milk, a combination he deemed fatal. I don't know if his ideas about milk are true, but he thought that he had verified them.

The first news I heard about that theory came to me under these circumstances. I was in the Saint James pastry shop, drinking my accustomed glass of cold milk, when in walked Capdevilla and shot a phrase at me that had the flavor of a biblical curse, since he usually expressed himself in memorable ways. "My dear Borges," he said, "you are drinking in your leprosy." I let go of the glass immediately, somewhat alarmed, since his meaning was that with the milk I was drinking, I was predestined for leprosy. Later he explained his theory to me, which he had expounded upon in one of his books on medicine.

Capdevilla asserted that all sickness had a dietetic origin, and that there are foods which are extremely dangerous. I remember at his home how he used to prepare a great salad of vegetables and fruits. He was the only one in his family who ate such food, since he had not managed to convince his family, which preferred a square meal. Loyal to his theories, Capdevilla ate those dishes, and I believe that he kept in excellent health until the day of his inevitable death.

ALIFANO: Borges, you were a close friend of Capdevilla. Could you talk about your relationship with him? What was he like? What sort of relationship did he have with his family?

BORGES: A normal relationship, certainly. Except that his family would laugh a little at him, and they would joke about his desire to be a purist in his speech. He spoke in a very Spanish manner. It is said that in Spain he would speak in this way with such devotion that not even the Spaniards themselves understood him. Capdevilla had read many nineteenth century authors and used phrases which now are anachronisms, not only here in Argentina but in Spain itself. For example, I frequently heard him say: " Vive Dios!" (God be witness!), a phrase that we have all read in old Spanish texts; in Cervantes, for instance: " Vive Dios que espanta esta grandeza!" (God be witness that this greatness horrifies!). But, of course, not even in Spain have I ever heard anyone use that phrase. Now, as I said, Capdevilla spoke somewhat like the characters of the nineteenth-century Spanish novel or theatre, and this led not only his family but people in general to look upon him with a certain amusement.

ALIFANO: The fact that Capdevilla spoke a pure Spanish was, undoubtedly, a sign of the devotion he had for Spain and for all Spanish literature, wasn't it?

BORGES: Yes. A rather indiscriminate devotion, which I, of course, do not share, and which I discussed with him many times. It seems to me that in the history of Spanish literature there are some remarkable writers and others who, well, are simply abominable. Capdevilla, however, as you have noted, admired with devotion all Spanish literature.

ALIFANO: How did you meet Capdevilla? Do you remember how you met for the first time, Borges?

BORGES: How odd. No, I don't remember how it happened—this has occurred with many friends and also with women I've been in love with. No, I can't remember how we met. Where could I have seen Capdevilla? He didn't have anything to do with the literary debates of the time. Nothing to do with the Martín Fierro literary group nor with *Proa* magazine, which Güiraldes, Rojas Paz, Brandan Caraffa and I edited. Capdevilla was seen as integral to the order of things. People saw him as a sort of institution, not as a person.

ALIFANO: When we started this conversation, you said Capdevilla's poem "*Aulo Gelio*" was a remarkable one. Can we talk about Capdevilla's poetry?

BORGES: Yes, of course. I would add that "*Aulo Gelio*" (Aulus Gellius) is not only the best poem by Capdevilla, it is also a perfect poem, one of the great poems of the Spanish language. From its opening lines it displays admirable balance and musicality: "*Aulo Gelio feliz bajo Elio Adriano,/ autor preclaro de Las Noches Aticas,/ que en plácidos inviernos escribiste,/ seguro de tu dicha y de tu fama*" (Aulus Gellius happy under Hadrian's rule,/ Illustrious author of The Attic Nights,/ You who in peaceful winters wrote,/ Assured of joy and fame). There is a balance in these verses which, unlike the balance in Quevedo's verses, is not strained, but natural and friendly. I could never forget the beautiful lines at the end of the poem. In them, Capdevilla catalogues the complete life of Aulus Gellius and finally says: "*Rompédme mi corona si la tengo!/ Arda mi vida en amistad humana,/ y algo sepa mi ciencia de los hombres,/ aunque no sepa de los dioses nada!*" (Smash my crown, if I possess one!/ Let my life blaze in human friendship,/ And let my craft know about men,/ Though it may lack all knowledge about gods!). That seems to me a memorable conclusion, because it arises after some impersonal verses referring to *The Attic Nights* and to certain aspects of that book of "*lección varia*" (diverse meaning), as people used to say in the old days. Now Capdevilla has books in which he mistakenly includes many patriotic romances commemorating almost all of Argentina's heroes. Capdevilla was also the occasional poet who trivialized his poetry. I don't know; perhaps he was aware of it.

ALIFANO: Did you see Capdevilla frequently?

BORGES: Of course, and I visited him often at his home. I remember this anecdote: on a certain occasion I was talking with him. It was around five o'clock in the afternoon. Suddenly, Capdevilla looked toward the dining room and said, "God be witness! The repast is served." That manner of speaking obviously was quite anachronistic in Buenos Aires. But rather than saying, "The tea is already served," he was used to expressing himself in that way. It is possible that if a writer is to write fluently in correct prose, he should become accustomed to speaking in a similar fashion. Perhaps Capdevilla's artificial manner of speaking was necessary to his style of writing.

Another theme that interested Capdevilla a great deal was the Orient, and he was particularly interested in theosophy. In this, he was much like

Güiraldes and Lugones. The three of them were interested in theosophy, and none of them was an orthodox Catholic. All three expounded upon the theme of the soul's immortality, telepathic communication and the transmigration of souls. So Capdevilla also had a great philosophical preoccupation aside from his scientific interests.

ALIFANO: So, as you've said, he was a man with a great curiosity, but did he deeply study those themes or was he superficially acquainted with them?

BORGES: I think that in many cases he was only superficially acquainted with them. Any theme obsessed Capdevilla in such a way that it could become a point of departure for him. Recently I visited England. I traveled with María Kodama, and we went to see Kipling's house and the library he had there. One of the things that struck me was that there were no literary works on the shelves, but rather travelogues, history books, books on India, books on naval and military history; many books on China, Japan and other Oriental countries. This demonstrates that to Kipling these works were points of departure; they were stimuli to write on any subject. Perhaps something similar was true of Capdevilla, and that is why many accuse him of being superficial. For Capdevilla, every book was a deep experience, as with Lugones. That is why one sees the influence of so many authors in Lugones. However, Lugones can imitate—or believes he is imitating—Hugo; he can imitate Laforgue, but he never stops being Lugones. There is something unmistakable about his style. Similarly with Capdevilla, but being a modest man, he did not want to be noisily personal. In spite of himself, however, he was.

I like to speak about Capdevilla, and I am pleased you suggested discussing him, because, as I said, he has been undeservedly disregarded. Capdevilla is not even attacked, which is also unfortunate. No one bothers to attack this great poet, perhaps for the reason we mentioned before: he did not belong to any movement. Capdevilla was clearly a *post-modernista* without trying to be one, and the models he followed were classical models. But I almost forgot to tell you something. I now remember that the only person who knew how to attack Capdevilla was the Argentine poet Arturo Mastronardi. I don't know why, but Mastronardi used the word "Capdevilla" as meaning a minimal measure; for example, "Do not have a Capdevilla of doubt." That, of course, was so unjustified that it was not harmful to Capdevilla. This is why I recall it; for I believe that Capdevilla was not demeaned in the least by that phrase. At any rate, it is an unquestionably ingenious phrase, and when a phrase is ingenious, it doesn't matter whether it is just or unjust.

15

Evaristo Carriego

Death was stalking him, and he knew it.

ALIFANO: In 1930 you published a book about Evaristo Carriego, that poet who first gave Argentine literature the theme of the *barrios* of Buenos Aires. Can we talk about Carriego, Borges?

BORGES: Yes, certainly. Carriego initiated a style when he discovered the pathetic and literary aspects of the suburbs of Buenos Aires. Carriego touched upon the epic possibilities of that theme, but later he concentrated more on its sentimental possibilities, which is somewhat similar to what happened with the tango. The tango went from the courage and daring of the *milonga* to the sung tango, which is sentimental and whining. I remember a *milonga* that was popular during my youth, and which went: "*Soy del barrio del Alto/ soy del barrio del Retiro./ Yo soy aquél que no miro/ con quién tengo que pelear*" (I am from the barrio del Alto/ I am from the barrio del Retiro./ I am one who never worries/ What guy I am going to fight). Or that other one that went: "*Soy del barrio de Montserrat,/ donde relumbra el acero,/ lo que digo con el pico/ lo sostengo con el cuero.*" (I am from Montserrat barrio,/ Where the steel blades gleam,/ What I speak out with my mouth/ I risk with my skin).

ALIFANO: Some of Carriego's poems, "*El guapo*" (The Tough), for example, are in that style that you like, isn't that so?

BORGES: Yes. And Carriego wrote that poem based on the life of Juan Muraña, a criminal from Palermo barrio. The poem, however, is dedicated to the memory of "Saint Juan Moreira," the Argentine gaucho who lived on the plains in a heroic manner. Carriego was a devotee of Juan Moreira, and he even dared to sanctify him. At the time, when one thought of the gauchos, the name of Juan Moreira would come up immediately. Now, however, people think of Martín Fierro. For example, I read the epic poem

83

Martín Fierro in what could be called a sort of clandestine manner, because when I told my mother that I wished to read it, she answered: "How can you think of reading that! That book is full of gross things." Then she advised me to go on reading Hilario Ascasubi or Estanislao del Campo, who according to her were the foremost pillars of the so-called *gauchesque* poetry. The canonization of Martín Fierro was the work of Leopoldo Lugones and it goes back to 1915, when he gave his famous lecture which later became his book *El Payador* (The Itinerant Singer).

ALIFANO: In your opinion, what aspect of the men of the barrios of Buenos Aires impressed Carriego?

BORGES: Without doubt, their courage. Carriego sings about valor, and his poetry captures all the epic possibilities of these men. "*Le cruzan el rostro, de estigmas violentos/ Hondas cicatrices, y tal vez le halaga/ Llevar imborrables adornos sangrientos:/ Caprichos de hembra que tuvo la daga*" (His face is violently branded with furrows/ Of deep knife scars, and perhaps he feels honored/ By so many indelible and bloody adornments/ Left by the dagger, whimsies of a woman). This refers to the medieval custom of seeing the warrior's sword as his woman, his deadly weapon. Remember also that the swords during medieval times had familiar names: Roland's sword is called "Durandall." In *The Song of Roland* there is a scene where he lies dying and, recalling all the campaigns they had undertaken together, he bids farewell to his sword. Some of those campaigns are evidently legendary, such as the conquest of Germany, the conquest of Scandinavia or the conquest of England. All that did not occur, but it doesn't matter. He bids farewell to his sword dreaming of those conquests. Now, one of the most beautiful farewells of a warrior to his sword is that described by Detlev von Liliencron, a German poet who fought in the war of 1870. He composed verses dedicated to a king who has been defeated and casts his sword into a river. And he says: "*In die Frieser trug er sein Schwert Hilfnot,/ das hat ihn heute betrogen*," which could be translated as "Against the Dutch he carried his sword Hilfnot,/ and she has betrayed him today." That is, the sword has been unfaithful to him, has betrayed him. This has the same sense as the "whimsies of a woman" that Carriego attributes to the dagger.

ALIFANO: How did you meet Evaristo Carriego?

BORGES: Thanks to my cousin, Alvaro Melián Lafinur, and to Marcelo del Mazo. The latter is a great writer who has been unjustly forgotten and who felt for Carriego that almost perplexed admiration which a man of letters often feels for an intuitive writer. They brought Carriego to my house. Carriego and I were neighbors. I remember that he was a slight, dark man who had the burning eyes that all consumptives have. Carriego died from tuberculosis, and I believe that he was aware that he had that disease. Perhaps that is why he continually spoke about his work and wrote incessantly. Death was stalking him, and he knew it. Carriego had devoted himself to death and knew that he had no possibility of immortality except in his written words; that is why he was so impatient to achieve glory. He would compel people to hear his verses at the café, or he would lead the conversation toward themes that he wrote about. I believe that his need to have people remember him had a tyrannical hold on him. I can't remember right now who decided at the time that Almafuerte, Lugones and Enrique Banchs already comprised the triumvirate of Argentine poetry. Then Carriego stormed the cafés to propose the deposition of Lugones, so that Lugones would not be an obstacle to his own inclusion in the threesome.

ALIFANO: Was Evaristo Carriego a friend of your family?

BORGES: Well, the Borges family and the Carriego family had known each other back in the province of Entre Ríos. And Carriego met my father again here, in Buenos Aires. In my house there was a book by Carriego with a dedication to my father that read: "To my compatriot in the Republic of Entre Ríos, Doctor Jorge Borges." My father was born in that province. One night, Carriego, in that grandiloquent tone he had, said to my father: "Here we are, the two from Entre Ríos." My father answered in a quieter tone: "Yes, and like all persons from Entre Ríos who can manage to get out, here we are in Buenos Aires."

ALIFANO: Carriego used to visit you on Sunday afternoons, after coming from the horse races, isn't that so, Borges?

BORGES: Yes, and Carriego was almost always accompanied by Doctor Alfredo Palacios, Macedonio Fernández, Marcelo del Mazo, my cousin Alvaro Melián Lafinur and a Swiss poet who Rubén Darío occasionally mentioned: Charles de Soussens. We called him Charles de Sans Sous, meaning without a cent. Those Sunday gatherings would last until the late hours of the night. They dined in my house, and then they talked and sometimes argued until dawn. Soussens was a great friend of Carriego and Carriego liked him and disliked him for the same reasons. He was fond of Soussens's culture, his identity as a Frenchman who had assimilated the prestige of Dumas, Verlaine and Napoleon; but he was at the same time bothered by his being a *gringo*, a foreigner, a man born without ancestors, without dead relatives in the Americas. Now, I believe that Carriego secretly admired Soussens. A frequent phrase in Carriego's conversation was, "The night that Soussens discovered me."

ALIFANO: I understand that many of Carriego's friends were characters from the barrios—criminals. A boss of the barrios, Nicolás Paredes, whom you met, was a friend and protector of Carriego, wasn't he, Borges?

BORGES: It's true. He was the friend he saw most frequently and who was closest to him. Nicolás Paredes, who at the time was the boss of the Palermo barrio, loved him and cared for him like a son. Carriego, even before he was fifteen, had sought his friendship. He asked around for the name of the local caudillo and went to see him, making his way through the thugs in their tall hats, who acted as praetorian guards to the caudillo Paredes. When Carriego was before him he said, "I am Carriego, from Honduras Street." Once he was accepted, he rubbed elbows with thugs and killers of every sort, confidently calling those assassins by their first names. I also met Paredes and became his friend. But by then he had retired.

ALIFANO: What led you to meet don Nicolás Paredes?

BORGES: Well, it was because of the book I wrote about Carriego. I had been awarded the Second Municipal Prize for Literature; the most important prize that I've ever received, the one that moved me the most since it was the first one I was awarded. That distinction provided me with three thousand pesos, an amount that allowed me to spend a year without holding a job, and allowed me to write in my house, at leisure, that book on Carriego. I remember that I went to see Félix Lima, the first writer who ever wrote in slang and in the Spanish spoken by the Jews; he was the one who popularized that phrase "*Qui mi cointas* " (What's happening?), frequently used by the Jews. I went to see Félix Lima because he had been a close friend of Carriego, and he then advised me to visit don Nicolás Paredes. And so I became a friend of Paredes. Unfortunately, Paredes never saw my book because he died in 1929, and the book appeared in 1930.

But I am going to tell you something very intimate about Evaristo Carriego, something I've never told anyone before: I am going to dare to tell you about a poem that Carriego dedicated to my mother and that refers to me. The poem is entitled "*Vulgar Sinfonía*" (A Vulgar Symphony) and carries this dedication by Carriego: "To doña Leonor Acevedo de Borges." And then it refers to me in verses which I don't know if they are prophetic, at any rate they are not very successful: "And your son, that child/ Of your pride who already begins to feel on his head/ The slight touch of the laurel wreath."

ALIFANO: What importance does Carriego have for Argentine literature, Borges?

BORGES: I think that Carriego is more important to the history of our poetry, to the history of our literature, than to our literature itself. Personally, I owe much to Carriego. He was the one who revealed poetry to me when I was still very young. One night in my house Carriego stood and recited, in a grandiloquent manner, a long poem. I did not understand a word of it, but poetry itself was revealed to me, because I understood that words were not only a means of communication, but also that they contained a sort of magic. The poem was "*El misionero*" (The Missionary) by Almafuerte, and the verses that Carriego recited are still in my memory: "*Yo deliré de hambre muchos días/ Y no dormí de frío muchas noches/ Para salvar a Dios de los reproches,/ De su hambre humana y de sus noches frías*" (I was delirious with hunger many days/ And I was cold and slept not a wink many nights/ To save God from suffering unjust reproaches,/ From his human hunger and his cold nights).

16

Cervantes

> ... one can see that Cervantes is so
> moved when he says goodbye to our
> friend and his friend [Don Quixote] that
> he hesitates, and finally ends with those
> words, "That is to say, he died," rejecting
> all rhetoric. Cervantes is deeply and
> sincerely moved when he is left alone.

ALIFANO: Borges, you once confessed that you have read very few novels. One that you have read is *Don Quixote*, the second part of which you have often reread. Recently you wrote an introduction to an Italian translation of *Don Quixote de la Mancha*. Wouldn't this be a good time to talk about that piece, and, for that matter, about Cervantes's masterpiece?

BORGES: Yes, I have just finished writing that introduction, and while I was doing it, I noticed several things about Cervantes's novel. We can discuss them. In *Don Quixote* there are at least two stories: first, we have the obvious one, that is, the story of the "ingenious gentleman" himself; the other one, which has a deeper theme, and which I think is the central one, is the friendship between Don Quixote and Sancho Panza. This is a theme that has been used again and again in literature. Perhaps the foremost example is *Bouvard et Pécuchet* by Gustave Flaubert, where the most important element is the friendship between those two unfortunate characters. We also have a minor example in Argentine literature in Estanislao del Campo's *El Fausto*, where the true subject is not, as Lugones thought, the parody of Doctor Faustus but the friendship between the two companions. In *Don Quixote*, it seems to me that we can conceive of a third story. This idea has led me to imagine a story based on the last chapter of *Don Quixote*. I have not yet written the story and so I do not have much to disclose. I can only tell you that it will be the story of Alonso Quijano, who tried to become Don Quixote toward the end of his life. This would be a third theme.

As to the first one, the adventures that everyone knows, I remember that Juan Ramón Jiménez said that we could very well imagine Don Quixote undertaking different adventures, but that he would still be, essentially, Don Quixote. At present, however, the adventures are least interesting to me; I am much more interested in the two characters. And I am particularly interested, now that I am about to write a story featuring Don Quixote, in the character of Alonso Quijano, who wants to be Don Quixote at the end of his life.

ALIFANO: *Don Quixote* is a two-part novel. The first part—as many critics have said—is essentially different from the second part. At the beginning, Don Quixote and Sancho are two somewhat unexplained characters who get together and begin their adventures, receiving their expected share of jeers and beatings. In the second part all this changes; when the knight and his squire set out again, everyone knows who they are. Thus all the characters in the second part become accomplices in Don Quixote's madness. You have also pointed out that essential difference in a previous essay about Cervantes's great novel; moreover, you have confessed that you prefer the second part, isn't that so?

BORGES: Oh, yes, that is true. I believe that Cervantes wrote the second part ten years after the first. As you said, when they set out the second time, people already know them, and they all become accomplices in Don Quixote's madness. The most obvious example of this would be the episode of the Dukes. When Don Quixote and Sancho arrive at the palace, everything is ready for them, and a series of tricks is played on them to humor Don Quixote. Thus we have the episode of Clavileño, and we could also mention the bachelor Samson Carrasco, who, wishing to cure Don Quixote's madness, becomes the Knight of the Mirrors in order to defeat him. The fact that everyone humors Don Quixote makes the second part very different from the first.

ALIFANO: The saying "second parts are never good" is attributed to Cervantes. What a paradox, isn't it? Does it mean that Cervantes himself didn't have much faith in the second part of his novel?

BORGES: Well, it has been said that Cervantes was never too confident about the second part of *Don Quixote*. I think, however, that second parts have always been known to be good. In the second book, Cervantes dispenses with gross physical mishaps, and everything that happens is different. This book is sentimental, psychological; there aren't so many blows, so many beatings, and there are no longer those funny, terrible and yet imaginative incidents such as the adventure of the windmills. We could also say that when Cervantes began to write *Don Quixote* he knew very little about Alonso Quijano. Perhaps this is true of every book. When you start writing a book, you begin to relate to the characters. Paul Groussac has pointed out that the first book of *Don Quixote* is an exemplary novel similar to Cervantes's *"novelas ejemplares."* In the first part, Cervantes saw the comic possibilities of the action; in the second part, on the other hand, he saw the pathetic possibilities.

ALIFANO: Undoubtedly, that's the reason why the story develops differently and why the character also changes. Don't you think so?

BORGES: Yes. And in the final chapters we read about the knight's defeat in Barcelona, his return to his village, Sancho's kneeling down to thank God, and the death of Alonso Quijano. Undoubtedly, Cervantes regards Don Quixote's death as a very intimate and very sad event. It is sad for the reader and sad for Alonso Quijano, who dies confessing that he has not been Don Quixote. It is particularly sad for Cervantes, who narrates the death of his character in these words: "And amidst the tears and lamentations of his friends, he gave up the ghost; that is to say, he died." You see, at that point one is expecting a literary phrase, an ambitious phrase such as Shakespeare's words on Hamlet's death. But no; one can see that Cervantes is so moved when he says goodbye to our friend and his friend that he hesitates, and finally ends with those words, "that is to say, he died," rejecting all rhetoric. Cervantes is deeply and sincerely moved when he is left alone.

ALIFANO: The opening lines of *Don Quixote* are also remarkable. One immediately senses one is in the presence of a great writer. Do you agree, Borges?

BORGES: I do. I believe those opening lines must be studied by those of us who write stories. I have them memorized; I have never forgotten them, and I must tell you I learned them when I was very young: "At a village of La Mancha, whose name I do not wish to remember, there lived a little while ago one of those gentlemen who are wont to keep a lance in the rack, an old buckler, a lean horse and a swift greyhound." That opening sentence is remarkable. When you begin to read a book, you are immersed in your everyday world, and then you have to remove yourself to another world, the world of the book. That long opening sentence seems very successful to me because when you read it you forget the things around you. I read that sentence and find myself immersed in the world that Cervantes presents to us.

ALIFANO: I don't know if you remember that in his essay about *Don*

Quixote, Paul Groussac, referring to the first chapter, says that it seems cruel to remind us that Cervantes had more time to polish his style because he wrote that part in jail.

BORGES: Well, Groussac will excuse me, but I have reached a different conclusion; I don't think that circumstance had much to do with Cervantes's style. Perhaps *Don Quixote*'s effectiveness is, above all, due to something we might call Cervantes's voice—a kind and natural voice. Very often he tells us superfluous things, relatively unimportant things that may not add much to the story, but he tells them to us with affection. Cervantes dwells on certain things that in themselves are not very inventive, but you feel that he is always attentive to his surroundings, that he does not deceive us at any point. Cervantes is always seeing—with the eye of the imagination, that is—everything he tells us. And that is why we sense that Cervantes is fond of little novelties: he notes that the Knight of the Green Coat is wearing a green riding coat; he gives us a detailed description of Don Quixote's house. Cervantes presents all this with indulgence and, above all, with affection, yet at the same time, with a certain irony.

ALIFANO: Borges, would you say that *Don Quixote*'s immortality could be attributed to what you have just said about its author?

BORGES: Yes. I believe it could be attributed, above everything else, to Cervantes's voice. But I am going to say something else about *Don Quixote* which could also be said about *Hamlet*, and which would perhaps be better explained through the latter: We all believe in Prince Hamlet, in Polonius, in Ophelia; we can also believe in the king. However, we do not believe in Hamlet's story. The reason is that Shakepeare would use any old story, and then he would develop it to suit his needs. Bernard Shaw said that in Shakespeare's work one must always distinguish between the stories, which are terrible, and the characters, who are not. It is impossible, for instance, to believe in the last act of *Hamlet*, in which all the major characters are killed. But we do believe in Hamlet. Hamlet is an eternal character in the memory of the human race. So is Don Quixote. In my introduction, I say that we can imagine that, as centuries go by, all copies of *Don Quixote* may well disappear, but I am sure that the image of the knight and his squire will never be forgotten, because those characters have become a part of the memory of mankind.

17

Dante

> I would say that [by reading *The Divine Comedy*] we almost know Dante as well as did Virgil, who was a dream of his; and undoubtedly more than his mistress and muse, Beatrice Portinari, was able to know him.

ALIFANO: Borges, you have said on several occasions that few texts have given you as much pleasure as *The Divine Comedy*, which you have read in several translations.

BORGES: Yes, I have read all the editions of *The Divine Comedy* that I have come upon, and spent a long time studying the diverse commentaries and the different interpretations of that magnificent work. I don't know Italian; I never studied that beautiful language, but I can tell you that through Dante I learned a great deal of Italian. Later came Ariosto, another writer that increased my liking and delight in that language. So that I could say that I owe all the Italian that I know and admire to the *Comedy* and to *Orlando Furioso*.

ALIFANO: What differences did you notice in the commentaries of the various editions of the *Comedy*?

BORGES: I noticed that in the oldest versions a theological commentary is predominant; then, particularly in the nineteenth century, there was a historical commentary or interpretation; and at present I believe that the aesthetic commentary predominates, especially in the editions of Grabher and Momigliano. These commentators pay attention to the metrics of each line, an element which to me is one of Dante's greatest virtues. But Dante possesses a quality on which I place a special emphasis: the tenderness, the refinement and the delight that some passages of the *Comedy* have. We generally think of the Florentine poem as somber and sententious, and we forget the tenderness often found in the plot. Undoubtedly, Dante must have read a book on the geometry of the time; it must have been the source of his observation that the four-square is the most firm of all shapes; a scientific observation of the time that has nothing poetic about it. However, Dante uses it with a metaphor relating to the man who knows how to bear misfortunes. *"Ben tetragono ai colpi di ventura,"* he says in that famous line, which could be translated as: "Four-square against the hammering of chance."

ALIFANO: In relation to what you are saying, I recall that odd metaphor of the arrow.

BORGES: Yes. Dante wants to speak of the quickness, of the speed of the arrow as it comes from the bow and hits the target. He tells us then, to show us how quickly that action happens, that the arrow pierces the target and then comes from the bow, leaving the cord behind. In other words, he inverts the beginning and the end of the action to show its quickness. There is another line that I often recall: the one in the first canto of *Purgatory*, where Dante describes that incredible morning in the mountain. There, he says, after having emerged from the sadness, from the horror of hell: *"Dolce color d'orïental zaffiro, / che s'accoglieva nel sereno aspetto / del mezzo, puro infino al primo giro."* Dante, in those lines, tells us that he has just finished cleansing himself of all irreparable sadness and of that terrifying smoke, and he does this by describing the dawn; he compares the color of the dawn with an oriental sapphire.

ALIFANO: The beginning of the *Comedy* is evidently a dream of Dante, an observation you stated in your recent work, *Nueve ensayos dantescos* (Nine Dantesque Essays). However, in the last pages of *Paradise*, the *Comedy* can represent many things. This is what gives it its quality as a masterpiece, isn't that so?

BORGES: Obviously. The beginning of the *Comedy*, as you have just recalled, is a dream of Dante; and Dante in turn is only the object of that dream. Dante tells us that he doesn't know how he ended up in that dark forest *"tant'era pien di sonno a quel punto"* (My sleep was so leaden at that instant). The *sonno* is a sort of metaphor for the obfuscation of a sinful soul, but it also suggests the indefinite beginning of the act of dreaming. Then certainly, in its final pages, the *Comedy* reaches many levels of meaning; I would say all levels. The sublime, the grandiose, the universal is achieved by Dante and his work becomes part of the memory of mankind.

ALIFANO: What is your opinion of Benedetto Croce's contention that the *Comedy* sustains itself, never falters, mainly because of the unique narrative style created by Dante?

BORGES: I agree with that. I remember that when I was young the narrative style was scorned; it was called the "anecdotal manner," and people would forget, or would not take into account, that poetry originated as narrative. The roots of poetry, moreover, are found in the epic, and the epic is the primordial poetical genre; the epic encompasses time; in the epic we find a before, a now, and an after. In his *Comedy*, Dante introduces us to the narration in an almost magical way. That is why I would advise the reader to forget, let's say, the hatreds between the Guelfs and the Ghibellines, to forget scholasticism, to forget even the inclusion and the allusions to mythology or to Virgil's verses (which Dante perfects and frequently evokes since they are magnificent Latin verses). Let the reader forget all that and allow himself or herself to be carried along by the narrative. As I've said, I have read *The Divine Comedy* many times, and I have always let myself be carried by the act of reading the narrative, by the aesthetic emotion which every turn of the page gave me. The commentaries, critiques, all that must be left for later.

ALIFANO: That narrative, moreover, is affable, always elegant and gentle. When Dante talks of the supernatural, he doesn't need to prepare the reader, for it comes with such remarkable naturalness.

BORGES: True. Dante doesn't need to prepare the reader. "*Nel mezzo del cammin di nostra vita/ mi ritrovai per una selva oscura.*" Dante tells us that in the middle of his life he found himself in the midst of a dark forest, which is, of course, allegorical, but in whose physical presence we believe. The Psalms advise that a prudent man should wait until he is seventy to enter those secrets of the universe; Dante reveals to us in his narrative that at thirty-five ("*Nel mezzo del cammin di nostra vita*") a vision comes to him. I don't believe that Dante was a visionary; a vision is something more fleeting, something more ethereal. A vision as prolonged as *The Divine Comedy* is impossible. I think that his vision was voluntary. His vision was the result of his poetic faith—but that would be a theme in itself, a very interesting one which should be pursued.

ALIFANO: You probably remember that Coleridge said that poetic faith is the willing suspension of disbelief.

BORGES: Yes. It seems to me a correct notion. For example, if we watch a play, we know that on the stage we are seeing people in disguise who repeat the words that, for example, Shakespeare, Pirandello or Ibsen have put in their mouths. Yet, we believe that those are not men in disguise; we accept that that gentleman who soliloquizes hesitantly on the verge of vengeance is truly Hamlet, the prince of Denmark. We abandon ourselves to it. In films that process is even more curious, because we are no longer seeing disguised people, but rather photographs of them; and yet we believe in them as long as the film lasts. This illusion of reality, in Dante's case, is so vivid, so precise, that we come to suppose that he truly believed in his other world—in that world imagined by his poetic vision, by his poetic faith. And so we feel it as real, just as real as he himself felt it.

ALIFANO: Dante also leads us to know him deeply, doesn't he?

BORGES: Yes, and he achieves that by writing in the first person; a practice which is not a mere grammatical exercise as some people believe. Dante says *I saw* rather than *they saw*, or *it was*. This includes Dante as a character in the *Comedy*. This was a new development in literature at that time.

ALIFANO: Saint Augustine also wrote his *Confessions* in that manner.

BORGES: Yes, but those *Confessions*, by their splendid rhetoric, do not come as close to us as Dante does in his *Comedy*. The African's rhetoric comes between what he wants to say and what we hear. That rhetorical vice is very common to many writers. Rhetoric should act as a bridge, a road, but generally it is a wall, an obstacle. That can be seen in such different writers as Seneca, Quevedo, Milton, Lugones; in all of them, what they say comes between them and us.

ALIFANO: This doesn't happen with Dante, particularly because he allows us to know him, isn't that so?

BORGES: True. And he reveals himself to us in a more personal manner than his contemporaries. I would say that we almost know Dante as well as did Virgil, who was a dream of his; and undoubtedly more than his mistress and muse, Beatrice Portinari, was able to know him. I believe that through the *Comedy* we come to know Dante better than anyone else. Dante stands before us, he leads us, he is the center of the action. Things that happen around him are not only seen by him, but he is also part of them. The part he plays is not always in accord with what he describes, but I believe this is of slight importance. Thus, we have Dante terrified by hell (he must be terrified, and one feels that in the description, not because he is a coward, but because it is necessary for him to be terrified for us to believe in hell). We feel that he is afraid. The poet then goes on to give us his opinions on things. These opinions come through not because he tells us so, but rather because of the poetic feeling that comes from his description, by the cadence of his language, by its musicality and tone.

ALIFANO: Borges, in the *Comedy* we have two main characters who make their presence felt: Dante, and Virgil, who, as you say, was a dream of Dante's. These two characters are friends. So that this work, in a different manner than others, deals with a central theme in the literature of all times: the theme of friendship.

BORGES: That friendship, as you point out, is treated in a unique manner in the *Comedy*. Dante is a friend of Virgil's, moreover, Dante is like a son to Virgil; but, at the same time, Dante is superior to Virgil because he believes himself to be saved. He believes that he will deserve such a blessing, or that he has deserved it since he was granted a vision of it. On the other hand, at the beginning of the *Inferno*, Dante knows that Virgil is a damned soul, and the very moment that Virgil tells him that he will not be able to accompany him beyond purgatory, Dante feels that Virgil will always be an inhabitant of that *"nobile castello"* where the great shadows of the great men of antiquity dwell, those that through unavoidable ignorance did not accept or could not reach the word of Christ. At that moment, Dante says to Virgil: *"Tu, duca; tu, signore; tu, maestro."* To cover up that horrible moment, Dante salutes him with the highest epithets and speaks of the great love and the long study to which Virgil's writings have led him, and of their relationship which has always been constant. But Virgil is sad since he knows that he is condemned to the *"nobile castello,"* far from salvation and full of God's absence; Dante, on the other hand, will see God, he will be *allowed* to, and he will also be allowed to understand the universe. So the theme of friendship is there, in a unique way, as you've pointed out, and we can relate it to other famous friendships: Don Quixote and Sancho, Huck Finn and the black man, Kim and the lama, Martín Fierro and Cruz, and so on, the list is endless.

ALIFANO: I recall that I've heard you say that the *Comedy* is the highest work of literature, of all literatures. Do you still hold that opinion, Borges?

BORGES: Yes, certainly. The *Comedy* has given me highly intense aesthetic emotions; it is a book that all of us must read. Not to read the *Comedy* is to deprive ourselves of the greatest gift that literature can give us. Dante, moreover, is one of the most extraordinary personages in all of literature. I always say that I read for pleasure, that I seek emotion in books. The emotion that I have felt in my many readings of the *Comedy* will be with me until my end; it is an emotion that goes beyond my wakeful hours.

18

Ricardo Güiraldes

> ALIFANO: It has been said that you personally knew the gaucho who inspired Güiraldes. What was Don Segundo Sombra like?
>
> BORGES: ... Don Segundo was not a hoodlum but a working man who did not bother anyone. The famous hoodlums could not understand why Güiraldes had based his book on that "wretch."

ALIFANO: How did you happen to meet Ricardo Güiraldes?

BORGES: I met him in a hotel that was on Maipú Street between Córdoba and Viamonte Streets. Brandan Caraffa introduced me to him. Brandan wanted to found a literary journal, *Proa*, and he came to tell me he had talked with Pablo Rojas Paz and with Ricardo Güiraldes and that they had decided to create a magazine, from which I could not be left out. That publication was to meet the needs of the new literary generation. I, of course, was very flattered with their attitude toward me. And I said to my mother: "By God, this is wonderful! They've told me that I couldn't be missing from a magazine for young writers that some of my friends are creating with Güiraldes. This is really gratifying." My mother agreed completely with my opinion, and Brandan Caraffa and I went the next day to the hotel where Güiraldes was staying.

ALIFANO: What year did that take place?

BORGES: My dates are vague, but it must have been around 1924 or 1925. Ricardo Güiraldes was older than I by ten or twelve years; of course, to a young man, ten years are a lot, although later it is the same to be sixty or seventy, seventy or eighty. Güiraldes was, indeed, what people called back then *"un escritor de fuste"* (a writer of consequence). I remember that at the meeting he said to us: "I am older than you are, young men, and I am really moved that you have met with Brandan Caraffa" (with Caraffita, as he used to call him affectionately), "and that you have decided that a magazine for young writers cannot be published without my collaboration." I understood then that behind all that was Brandan Caraffa's scheme to bring out the magazine. At that point, Pablo Rojas Paz arrived and my suspicions were confirmed. "I am very flattered," said Rojas Paz, "by this honor that you do me. . . ." And I interrupted him: "Yes, a few days ago Ricardo Güiraldes, Brandan Caraffa and I met and agreed that a magazine for young writers could not manage without someone like you." Güiraldes, who understood the scheme, winked at me, Brandan Caraffa laughed, and a short time later *Proa* appeared.

ALIFANO: Where did the funds for *Proa* come from?

BORGES: Well, each of us gave fifty pesos. But I suspect that the magazine cost much more than the amount we gave. I think Güiraldes added the necessary funds to cover the cost of production. Güiraldes was a very generous man, and he was always willing to donate money for all cultural enterprises, especially if those projects were supported by young people.

ALIFANO: Güiraldes was a man in love with the Argentine pampa, despite the fact that he came from Buenos Aires, indeed, was born right in the downtown area of Buenos Aires.

BORGES: Yes, he was born in his parents' home (people used to be born in their own homes in the old days), and this house was in the very center of downtown, between Florida and Paraguay Streets. He spent his childhood and adolescence there, but he used to travel frequently to San Antonio de Areco, where his family had a ranch. Later, Güiraldes bought an apartment in Solís Street, close to Congreso Plaza, where we used to visit him. One of the things I remember about that apartment was the large library Güiraldes had there. That library had two sections: One of its wings had books by French and Belgian Symbolists and a smattering of Argentine authors; the works of Leopoldo Lugones were there; also works by Poe translated into French. The other wing had books on theosophy. Güiraldes was interested in those ideas, and, like the rest of us at that time, he was also a devoted reader of Lugones.

His writing was influenced by Lugones. We used to speak ill of Lugones, but deep down we felt that to write well was to write like Lugones. I think that influence is noticeable in Güiraldes's novel *Don Segundo Sombra*. The range of his essay *El payador* (The Itinerant Singer) encompasses a more complex milieu, one that goes back to that time in Argentine history known as "The Conquest of the Desert." In the work of Lugones many events take place; in *Don Segundo*, on the other hand, few events take place other than the theme of friendship. I remember that I gave a copy of *Don Segundo* to my friend, the boss of the Palermo district, Nicolás Paredes, who had been the protector of Evaristo Carriego. A few days later, I asked him what he thought of Güiraldes's book, and he, perhaps because of his loyalty to the novels of Eduardo Gutiérrez or to *Martín Fierro*, denied that he liked it. He said to me: "Tell me, Borges, when does that *criollo* fight? I kept on turning the pages expecting a bloody fight, but it never happened." There is a complete literary definition in that, don't you think? Paredes wanted a book full of action, with knife duels, which is why *Don Segundo* disappointed him so much.

ALIFANO: *Don Segundo* is a sort of elegy that gives the impression that everything is happening for the last time, don't you think so?

BORGES: Yes, I do. And perhaps Güiraldes felt that more than anybody else. It's true; everything happens in that book as though it were happening for the last time. There is a breaking in of horses, and one feels that it is the last breaking in of horses; there is a cattle drive, and one feels that it is the last cattle drive. Everything happens for the last time. Güiraldes is a *criollo* gentleman who seems to be bidding farewell to everything with an habitual courtesy. He says goodbye, with evident nostalgia, to that world which was disappearing, to that world which was slowly dying out. I have attempted to classify *Don Segundo* by suggesting that it is not a novel, but an elegy, an admirable elegy.

ALIFANO: I am sure that one social circumstance that influenced Güiraldes was that, in the area where he had his ranch, Italian and Spanish immigrants had begun to establish farms that were progressively displacing the gaucho.

BORGES: Ah, yes, around that time agricultural farms began to flourish, which meant that the *criollo* world, the world of the gaucho, was disappearing from the countryside. Now, of course, many people say that at no point in that book are farms mentioned. Well, one could answer that *Don Segundo* is not an historical novel, nor does it intend to be realistic. Güiraldes's book is conceived as an elegy about that old world of cattlemen. That is why there are no references to new things. Like all elegies, *Don Segundo* ends by bidding farewell, and that brings to mind an analogous passage in *El payador*, where Lugones speaks of the gaucho who leaves with his poncho fluttering in the wind and with a flag at half mast. I think that Güiraldes echoed that passage intentionally to remind us of Lugones, since he was a devoted admirer of Lugones.

ALIFANO: It has been said that you personally knew the gaucho who inspired Güiraldes. What was don Segundo Sombra like?

BORGES: Yes, I met that gaucho, who was called Segundo Ramírez

Sombra. He was a heavy-set and relatively short man, and was quite intro-verted. An employee of the National Library—the son of a cattle driver whom Güiraldes mentions in the prologue to his book—told me that the hoodlums of San Antonio de Areco, jealous because the book was dedi-cated to don Segundo, disliked him intensely. The Toro Negro and his son the Torito, who were famous local hoodlums and who had been body-guards to Güiraldes's father, were the ones who hated the poor man most. When those bullies would come into a tavern, don Segundo would flee through the back door—he was afraid of them. Don Segundo was, more-over, a foreigner in that region, since he was born in the province of Santa Fé. Don Segundo was not a hoodlum but a working man who did not bother anyone. The famous hoodlums could not understand why Güiraldes had based his book on that "wretch."

ALIFANO: Güiraldes was a man who had a profound knowledge of all aspects of rural life.

BORGES: Yes, Güiraldes knew all the secrets of the countryside. He was also a guitar player and singer. Güiraldes spent hours singing and talking. I'll tell you something I have not told anyone before: Güiraldes often came to my house for lunch. He would arrive around ten in the morning, and after lunch, he would delight us with his guitar playing and his *milongas*. One day as he was bidding farewell, my mother pointed out that he was leaving his guitar behind. And Güiraldes answered her, "I did it on purpose, doña Leonor. As I told you, I am leaving for France next Saturday, and I wanted something of mine to remain with you." So that for six or seven months we kept in our house the guitar of Ricardo Güiraldes.

19

Nathaniel Hawthorne

Hawthorne set himself apart from any
relation with the world—he isolated
himself voluntarily, as he says—so that
literature would not lack that unique
story of the obsessed Wakefield.

ALIFANO: Borges, you say in an essay that the Spanish writer and philosopher José Ortega y Gasset can reason, well or poorly, but that he cannot imagine; and that Nathaniel Hawthorne, on the other hand, a man of continual imagination, rejects reason. That is to say, he thinks in images, in intuitions, "as women are able to do", you add, not through a dialectical process. I suggest that we talk about Hawthorne, whom you greatly respect, and whom you consider one of the great North American writers. Would you care to do so?

BORGES: Yes. And I thank you for reminding me of Hawthorne, an author whom I have always profoundly respected. I think that he is a creator of fables, which is not too bad. Now, an aesthetic error led him to append a moral to his fables, which often weakened them. I remember that in his notebooks statements such as these are found: Horrible things occur to a person; strange and mysterious things that keep him from being happy. He attributes all that to a secret enemy. Then he discovers that he is the only one to be blamed. The moral meaning, according to Hawthorne, is this: happiness lies within ourselves. Another: A man allows a snake to enter his stomach, where it feeds, tormenting him horribly. At the end of it, Hawthorne adds that it is a symbol of envy or of some other evil passion.

ALIFANO: These are plots of stories that Hawthorne wrote?

BORGES: Yes, they are plots found in his notebooks.

ALIFANO: Do you see that moral intention as something negative in the writing of fiction?

BORGES: No, I don't believe it is. Besides these were only notes, sketches

103

of stories, most of which he never wrote—as happens with almost all writers. Hawthorne was fascinated with these encounters, this contact with the imaginary. I think he spent his days imagining plots and thinking through images. Another rather odd sketch comes to mind: Two persons are in a street awaiting an event and the appearance of the main actors of that event. The event is already taking place and they are the actors, but they are not aware of it. I remember an even odder sketch: It deals with a writer (perhaps Hawthorne himself) who is writing a story and realizes that his characters do not obey him; that is, they act against his intention. Then things happen in a way unforeseen by him, and they approach a disaster he cannot avert.

ALIFANO: It's the clash of the plane of common reality with the aesthetic plane, isn't that so?

BORGES: That's true. It's the play between the real and the imaginary world; it's that world which in the act of reading we pretend is real. Hawthorne must have delighted himself with those fictional games. I think that first he imagined situations, perhaps involuntarily, and later sought the characters to embody them.

ALIFANO: He was a true creator of stories; a genuine storyteller.

BORGES: Yes, I suspect that all storywriters proceed in that manner. It happens also with Poe and sometimes with Henry James. I think that Melville, a great admirer of Hawthorne, did not proceed like that, neither did Conrad. If we take, for example, the adventures of Don Quixote, we find that they are not all that well conceived, likewise with Shakespeare's plots. But, at a deeper level, of what importance are the confused and unbelievable crimes and puerile scandals of the court of Denmark if we fully believe in Hamlet? Of what importance are the slow, antithetical and barely believable dialogues—"reasonings" as Cervantes himself calls them—of Don Quixote if we can believe in him? Furthermore, the authors of these characters have believed in them, have so deeply believed in them that they have rendered them believable.

ALIFANO: Hawthorne, as you have said, acted differently. That is, he first conceived of a situation or series of situations and afterward elaborated the characters required by his plot.

BORGES: Yes. As you have said, he was a true storyteller. By means of that method, it is possible to conceive admirable stories, since the plot is more obvious than the characters.

ALIFANO: That's not, however, the most appropriate way of writing novels, would you agree?

BORGES: True. In a novel the most important element is the characters—although I dislike Russian novels for their excess of characters. Besides, I think (and this was noted by Wells in the past century) that in every fantastic work there should be only one fantastic event, and not many of them. We see that in *The Invisible Man* there is only one invisible man. If there were more, the characters would seem unbelievable; whereas if there is only one it is acceptable. All the characters then appear real, or in any case, we can pretend they are real.

ALIFANO: Borges, can you, as a way of introduction to Nathaniel Hawthorne's life, talk about his famous story "Wakefield." I am interested in hearing you discuss his life since in it we can find some clues to his work.

BORGES: Yes, it seems an excellent idea. Malcolm Cowley sees in "Wakefield" an allegory of Hawthorne's reclusion. I can't remember well; I believe it was in 1804 that Hawthorne was born in the port of Salem, an old, decadent city with a biblical name. Four years later his father, Captain Hawthorne, died, and his widow, Nathaniel's mother, locked herself up in her bedroom; later his sisters did the same thing. So, from then on, those women cut off all communication and Nathaniel was cared for by a servant. Some years later, Hawthorne himself became a recluse in order to spend all his time reading, imagining and writing fantastic stories. More precisely, he revealed in a pathetic letter he wrote to Longfellow that he only went out walking at sundown. That reclusion lasted twelve years. And in the letter to Longfellow, Nathaniel Hawthorne says that he became a recluse without any intention of being one, and that he had realized later that he was a captive in a dungeon. "I cannot find the key to let myself out," he writes, "and if the door were open I should be almost afraid to come out."

ALIFANO: This would explain why upon reading the story about Wakefield in the newspapers Hawthorne would identify with him and would later write that remarkable short story.

BORGES: I think so. Hawthorne set himself apart from any relation with the world—he isolated himself voluntarily, as he says—so that literature would not lack that unique story of the obsessed Wakefield.

ALIFANO: You have also noted on previous occasions that Hawthorne's stories, written at the beginning of the nineteenth century, have a similarity in atmosphere and tone to Kafka's stories, created at the beginning of the twentieth century. Could you elaborate on that relation, Borges?

BORGES: Yes. "Wakefield" prefigures Kafka; I said this in a lecture I gave, I believe, in 1946 (my dates are vague). But I also said that Franz Kafka modifies and refines the reading of Hawthorne; it is a mutual debt, since a great writer creates his precursors and perfects them.

ALIFANO: There are many writers who prefigure Kafka. Kierkegaard also has a psychic affinity with the author of *The Castle*. Robert Browning's poem "Fears and Scruples" foreshadows Kafka's work. Hawthorne exemplifies Doctor Johnson's observation that no writer likes to owe anything to his contemporaries, isn't that so?

BORGES: Yes. Hawthorne ignored his contemporaries as much as possible. According to his biographers, he did not read, or more precisely, he refused to read De Quincey and Keats; nor did he read Hugo. And I believe that these authors never read him either. In 1964, when I was teaching at the University of Texas at Austin, I had access to Hawthorne's diaries, and I discovered in them that, like Stevenson, who was also the son of Puritans, he felt guilty for being a writer.

ALIFANO: Guilty for being a writer? Why?

BORGES: Well, perhaps he believed he should have fulfilled another destiny. To Hawthorne the writer's occupation was something frivolous and useless. I now remember that in the prologue of *The Scarlet Letter* he says that he imagines the ghosts of his ancestors looking at him as he writes his fictions. It is an odd passage. It is a dialogue between his ancestors, who have become shadows, whom he represents as gray shadows. One shadow asks: "What is he?" Another answers: "He is a writer of storybooks!" And then: "What kind of a business in life—what mode of glorifying God, or being serviceable to mankind in his day and generation—may that be? Why, the degenerate fellow might as well have been a fiddler!"

ALIFANO: It is sort of a revelation, isn't it?

BORGES: Yes. It is related to his intimate scruples. Hawthorne wrote morality tales and admirable short stories, and, because of the ancient dispute between ethics and aesthetics that must have weighed on him, he turned or tried to turn literature into a function of his conscience.

ALIFANO: Do you think that in pursuing such goals he weakened his work?

BORGES: No, not in the least. I believe that what matters is the end result. A writer may have absurd scruples, he may have banal or mistaken prejudices, but if his work is genuine, if it responds to the genuine vision of his dreams or of his imagination, he has fulfilled his work. This happens with Hawthorne, a writer who originates a manner of dreaming and makes us his heirs.

20

Rudyard Kipling

> He attributes everything to other
> people and to his good luck. He
> maintains that fate dealt him all the
> cards and all he had to do was to play
> them out. Which is untrue. Fate deals
> the cards to everyone, but if one is not
> Kipling those cards are wasted.

ALIFANO: You greatly admire Kipling. Many of us, guided by you, have read him and share the same admiration for him. You also have always defended him against those who found his politics deplorable.

BORGES: Well, it seems to me unjust to judge Kipling on the basis of his opinions of the British Empire. Kipling is one of the great literary geniuses of world literature.

ALIFANO: Well, how do you explain the unrestrained passion that he felt for the British Empire?

BORGES: I believe it can be explained if we bear in mind that he fervently believed in the British Empire, which he saw as a continuation of the Roman Empire. For Kipling, Rome and England were equivalent. That comes through in his short stories, for example, in "The Church That Was at Antioch," perhaps one of his best stories. In this story, a Roman soldier arrives in Antioch. Saint Peter and Saint Paul are characters in the story, yet one senses, at the same time, that the Roman soldier is a British officer serving in India. And there is another event, terrible, hateful, which shows the extent to which Kipling identified the two empires, chronologically so distant from each other: When his oldest son died in the First World War, among the first one hundred volunteers sent by England to France, he deplored such an unjust death and attributed this feeling to a father who has lost a son in the first century of our era. As I said, Kipling saw the British Empire as a continuation of the Roman Empire. But it is also important to note that he did not see this empire as guided by greed but rather by duty, and this he felt passionately.

ALIFANO: This passion is evident throughout his work. I remember, for example, that Kipling says: "What should they know of England who only England know?" Apparently, for him, it wasn't enough to know England: it was essential know the whole empire.

BORGES: And there's also a poem by Kipling in which he attacks soccer, and in which he refers to the English, not without spite, as "Little Englanders." Of course, he knew and had been born in that larger England, which is now dismembered, but which preserves in one way or another the English language and tradition. And he saw as his countrymen all inhabitants of "The Five Nations," as he called them: England, Canada, Australia, South Africa and India. Kipling's first book, dedicated to Bombay, where he was born, is titled *The Seven Seas* (that title, I suppose, was suggested by the magic of the number seven—the seven planetary gods, the seven capital virtues, the seven deadly sins); but in referring to "The Five Nations," he specifically mentions those parts of the empire that I've listed.

ALIFANO: Kipling also had a great love for France, didn't he?

BORGES: Yes, and he frequently mentioned it. Kipling saw France as the cultural center of the world. He extended his affection to all of Europe, but his great love was the British Empire. And that passionate love was fundamental to his life.

ALIFANO: Can that unrestrained attitude be justified in a man of genius, such as Kipling?

BORGES: I believe so. The British Empire did much good, as most empires do. We, for example, were shaped by the Roman Empire. And the evidence is that we speak a language which is an illustrious dialect of Latin. So I, for one, understand Kipling's attitude very well.

ALIFANO: What were Kipling's childhood and adolescence in India like?

BORGES: Quite tortured. It took him a long time to understand his condition, and I believe this marked him for life. Kipling arrived at the English language after having passed through Hindi; he had an Indian nurse who had taught him Hindi. Now, I don't know if he ever mastered Hindi or if he had only a spoken knowledge of it; most likely it was the latter. It seems unlikely he would have studied Hindi grammar. Of course, Kipling acquired, from an early age, a profound knowledge of English literature. And his vocabulary is very ample, in contrast, for example, to the vocabulary of Oscar Wilde—who wrote, moreover, in a much simpler form. Thus it's possible to read a story by Wilde, one of those delightful stories for children, and to understand it without any problem, but this is not so with Kipling, who is a highly complex writer.

ALIFANO: Does that complexity extend to all his work?

BORGES: Yes. There's a story by Kipling titled "The Gate of the Hundred Sorrows," which takes place in an opium den. I have read that story perhaps a hundred times during my life. And the last time it was read aloud to me I discovered something I had overlooked on previous occasions: the opium smoker, called Gabral Misquitta (Gabral is derived from the name Cabral, of distant Portuguese origin), tells the narrator the story of his life and refers to the story of the owner of an opium den. After a hundred readings, I noticed that Misquitta, who will die six weeks after having told that story, confuses his personal memories with the memories of the owner of the opium den. That detail, a very important one, I had never noted in all my previous readings. Rudyard Kipling was a consummate stylist and wrote with remarkable precision, allowing himself no obscurity, for that would have corrupted his style. His phrasing is perfectly crafted and only after many readings of one of his stories can one uncover its true meaning.

ALIFANO: I personally believe that Kipling, in contrast to other writers, was extremely complex but wanted to appear simple.

BORGES: That's true. And his early stories had a simple surface yet were highly complex—as complex as reality itself. Nevertheless, he tried as much as possible to be simple. Exactly the opposite of many present-day writers, who are appallingly simple but would like to seem complex.

ALIFANO: What is the most outstanding quality in Rudyard Kipling's work?

BORGES: His gift for storytelling. He possessed a quality rarely found in a writer. In "Ballad of East and West," Kipling tells a rather complex story (at least the two main characters are complex: the British officer and the Afghani who steals his horse). It is told in such a way that one hardly realizes that Kipling is performing miracles with rhyme and metaphor; one accepts it as a spontaneous act. However, it could not have been one, and undoubtedly he took great pains to achieve that illusion of spontaneity.

ALIFANO: Much has been made of Kipling's skepticism. Was he really a skeptic?

BORGES: Yes, I think so. And in his autobiography he dismisses everything he wrote. He says that *Kim* is a shamelessly picaresque work and that it doesn't have a plot. He also says that his mother always reproached him for his inability to invent plots. I disagree, however. *Kim* has a plot which is implicit in the characters, in the lama and in Kim himself. There is also the lama's vision, in which the reader sees that they have redeemed themselves; one through a life of meditation, the other through a life of action. Kipling created remarkable plots. I can't understand why his mother accused him of such a thing.

ALIFANO: That is a very odd autobiography, isn't it?

BORGES: It is. And Kipling, throughout the whole work, speaks modestly of himself, obviously unjustly. He attributes everything to other people and to his good luck. He maintains that fate dealt him all the cards and all he had to do was to play them out. Which is untrue. Fate deals cards to everyone, but if one is not Kipling those cards are wasted. There is another curious thing about Kipling which, as far as I know, has not been pointed out: he mastered every verse form. He carried out every sort of metrical experimentation including free verse, he invented many new forms, and yet in all his poetical works there is not a single sonnet. Perhaps he saw the sonnet as too intellectual, and therefore decided never to compose one. Shakespeare and Milton were the poets who used this form most frequently in England, and so Kipling perhaps thought that it was too presumptuous to do the same and avoided the sonnet. And there is yet another reason: Kipling wished to be a popular poet, and to write sonnets would have been, in a way, to betray that goal.

21

Quevedo and Lugones

A few days ago I was to deliver a
lecture on Lugones, and while I was
taking my nap, I dreamed I had to
lecture on Quevedo. That dream
suggests I find similarities between the
two writers.

ALIFANO: Borges, last year we celebrated the four hundredth anniversary of the birth of Don Francisco de Quevedo, that astonishing and living paradox who continues to evoke admiration and incite controversy. His vast work, despite "the partial glory that fate has strangely bestowed upon him" as you have said, will not be forgotten, not even lessen. Didn't you once confess that you couldn't imagine living a single day without recalling one of Quevedo's sonnets?

BORGES: Yes, I did. But the peculiar thing is that Quevedo has not become a universally known writer and that many literary directories even omit his name.

ALIFANO: Do you attribute that to the fact that Quevedo was not an affective but a formalist writer?

BORGES: Yes. For Quevedo words came before emotions. And as George Moore has pointed out, fame is usually awarded to maudlin literature. True, if one takes a good look at Quevedo's work or at his life, the sentimental element is lacking. Besides, he never created a symbolic character immortalized in people's imagination. Cervantes created Don Quixote and Sancho; Melville the white whale; Shakespeare Hamlet; Quevedo no one. What survived of him is his satiric images. He is a formalist writer and one has to conclude that he is *the* literary figure of the literati. One must be a man of letters in order to enjoy Quevedo. Notice that among Argentine writers we have a similar case, Leopoldo Lugones. Lugones too was a formalist writer whose main concern was words.

ALIFANO: That is a very interesting comparison between Quevedo and Lugones; could you elaborate?

BORGES: Yes. A few days ago I was to deliver a lecture on Lugones, and while I was taking my nap, I dreamed that I had to lecture on Quevedo. That dream suggests I find similarities between the two writers. Lugones, who was not particularly fond of Peninsular literature, felt great admiration for Quevedo. And I wrote in a poem: "*Quevedo, más castizo que Cervantes,/ Quevedo, flor de antologías, muere/ Como era entero en la coraza de su prosa./ Y no deja sucesión*" (Quevedo, more *castizo* than Cervantes,/ Quevedo, a perennial flower of anthologies, dies/ as he lived in the armor of his prose/ And leaves no heirs). We had Diego de Torres Villaroel, who invented some Quevedian devices, but he was only a second-rate writer. An American friend of mine says that it's a shame Spanish literature has forgotten Quevedo and remembered Góngora so well. I think that it would have been better for Spanish literature to have been the heir of Quevedo; not only because of the formalist aspect of his writing, but also because of his legacy as a thinker and moralist. Góngora, compared to Quevedo, is a mere decorative figure. Besides, Quevedo has a Spanish heritage, for two illustrious Spaniards were his ancestors—Seneca and Lucan.

ALIFANO: And to a great extent was Martial. Isn't it true, Borges?

BORGES: Ah, yes, Martial too. Quevedo learned much from him. Martial's epigrams were admirably translated by Quevedo.

ALIFANO: But let's return to your earlier point. Why do you say that it would have been better for Spain to receive the legacy of Quevedo rather than that of Góngora? Didn't Góngora come from the Spanish tradition as well?

BORGES: Not at all. Góngora's lineage is Italian. Besides, his poetry is no more than verbal artifice. I recall those verses of his that say: "*Plumas vestidos ya las selvas moran*" (Feather-dressed the jungles already dwelling). That line is completely absurd. "*Plumas vestidos*" cannot be said in Spanish. Maybe in Latin. In Spanish it should be "*vestidos de plumas*" (dressed in feathers). Then, "*las selvas moran*" (the jungles dwelling), is also absurd, because "*morar*" (to dwell) must be used as an intransitive verb and in this line it is used as a transitive one. In Spanish it should be "*morar en la selva*" (to dwell in the jungle). Here you have an obvious case of Latin nostalgia, which is found not only in Góngora, but also in many writers in other languages. Even in Lugones you find that; he wrote in a poem: "*El hombre numeroso de penas y de días*" (Man abundant in days and sorrows). That reads like Latin and feels like Latin.

ALIFANO: Borges, could you continue elaborating on your theory about the similarities between Quevedo and Lugones?

BORGES: Yes, certainly. With both of them you feel that each poem is a sort of verbal object, a verbal structure. That gets in the way of these two poets and their emotions, yet creates its own emotion. In Lugones, for instance, there is no intimacy; Lugones was a proud man. Each of his poems is a verbal object that lives beyond the author's intention. In Quevedo, however, there is a certain intended effect, but it doesn't quite become an emotion. Both are verbal writers. Well, all writers are ultimately verbal writers since their medium is words. But in Quevedo you notice the self-consciousness of each word, and the same is true of Lugones. Perhaps this is a fault. Think of Cervantes—his words are not noticeable. Cervantes possesses a flowing imagination carried away by the fable of Don Quixote and Sancho; for him words are a docile material. With Quevedo and Lugones, however, you feel there is an intelligence controlling the whole work; each word by these authors has been carefully chosen. Unfortunately, the reader feels the presence of the many revisions. The important thing is for the reader to feel that he is receiving something fresh, not a labored structure, which is what always happens with Quevedo and Lugones.

ALIFANO: You said that Quevedo never created a symbolic character that will live in people's imagination; neither has Lugones. But I would add something else, and I believe you are going to agree with me. It is not possible to link either author to only one of their books. They are scattered throughout all their literary works.

BORGES: It is true. Both authors are scattered, like the Pantheists' Devil. Reading only one of their books gives you an incomplete image; they are their complete works. Quevedo's work is very diverse. To me the greatest Quevedo is the author of *Las Musas* (The Muses), of *El Parnaso* (Parnassus) or *El buscón* (The Rogue). Quevedo's humor curiously anticipates that of Macedonio Fernández or Mark Twain. For example, remember those lines: "*Aquesto Fabio cantaba/ A los balcones y rejas/ De Aminta, que aún de olvidarlo,/ Le ha dicho que no se acuerda*" (This Fabio was singing/ At the balconies and windows/ Of Aminta, who, people have told him,/ Does not even remember to forget him). This anticipates Macedonio Fernández's style. Quevedo's presence can be felt in many authors. He was a writer who inhabited all genres with an implacable precision of language. To Quevedo, as I have said, language was a tool of logic. He would never have agreed with Chesterton, who maintained that language was not a scientific but an artistic medium, invented by warriors and hunters long before the beginning of science.

Quevedo (and in this he also resembles Lugones) always loathed stupidity. *Cuentos de cuentos* (Stories from Stories) is a work he created to expose ignorance. Quevedo was one of the best educated men of his time. The starting point of his memorable sonnets is often a classical work: for example, that line, *"polvo serán, más polvo enamorado"* (dust they will become, but dust in love), is an elaboration of a line from Propertius's *Elegy*, 1.19. *"ut meus oblito pulvis amore vacet"* (that my dust could be void and forgetful of love).

The range of styles of his poetry is very diverse: he even uses *"gongorismos"* to prove that he too is capable of constructing those verbal pyrotechnics. He proved it in those lines that read: *"Que a Jové fue disfraz, y fue vestido;/ Que un tiempo endureció manos reales,/ Y detrás de el los consules gimieron,/ Y rumia luz en campos celestiales"* (That which to Jove was costume and garment,/ That which at one time hardened royal hands,/ And behind which the consuls wept,/ And which ruminates light in the heavenly fields). These lines could have been written by Góngora, but they were written by Quevedo. His contemplative sonnets anticipate Wordsworth. And there is even a theological Quevedo. I remember those admirable lines: *"Con los doce cené: yo fuí la cena"* (I supped with all twelve: I was the dinner).

ALIFANO: What is the reason that the discovery of America is never mentioned in Quevedo's work nor in that of other Spanish writers?

BORGES: The reason is that Spaniards have not really felt the sea. For them the feeling of the sea is rather vague. The Portuguese, on the other hand, have felt it, as have the English and the Scandinavians. Spain is not a country of seamen. In *Don Quixote* one feels the plains of Castile: it is an inland book. Thus the discovery of America was somewhat ignored by Spaniards. Quevedo was a raging nationalist who never left Spain, except for that one adventurous trip to Italy. His phrase "Spain against all" is a warlike one. He believed the treasures that arrived from the Indies were responsible for making Spanish manners effeminate and causing heroic times to wane. I think that deep down he yearned for the medieval times when arms prevailed over letters, and he expressed it very well in the lines of a sonnet which read: *"Yace aquella virtud desaliñadad/ que fue, si menos rica, más temida,/ en vanidad y en ocio sepultada,"* (That unadorned virtue/ Which was, if less rich, more feared/ Lies buried in vanity and in sleep).

ALIFANO: It has been said that it took Quevedo fifteen years to write *Los sueños* (The Dreams). What do you think of that work, Borges?

BORGES: Well, I think that the last thing they resemble is dreams. I think that what he calls dreams are really satires. Dreams have a magical, mysterious quality that Quevedo's texts lack—that quality found in *Alice in Wonderland* by Lewis Carroll. I suspect that Quevedo never dreamed, and that he did not seek the realm of dreams, which is generally inhabited by the uncertain and the illogical. Perhaps Quevedo, who had the habit of reasoning, scorned the realm of dreams. I have said that there are no emotions in his work, and it is very possible that for that reason he could not enter the realm of dreams. A sonnet comes to mind which Quevedo dedicated to the memory of Don Pedro Girón, Duke of Osuna, who died in prison. That sonnet conveys no feeling. It is like an official monument, endowed with its own existence, which Quevedo erects beyond the Duke of Osuna—who is remembered thanks to that sonnet and is best forgotten because of his low-minded deeds.

ALIFANO: You have mentioned Quevedo as one of your masters. In which way did Quevedo's work most influence Jorge Luis Borges?

BORGES: I would say in every possible way. I have spent my life rereading Quevedo. Many of my friends have done the same thing. I remember someone once asked Macedonio Fernández: "What do you think of Góngora?" And he answered: "I don't sleep on that side." Then he added: "Quevedo and Mark Twain keep me awake."

ALIFANO: Borges, why hasn't Quevedo been translated into other languages?

BORGES: Because he is a verbal writer. The way he says things is more important than what he says. In order to gain international recognition it is perhaps more desirable to be less perfect. If form is all there is, it cannot be rendered into another language. Take Shakespeare, on the other hand, who is also a formalist, yet who offers other elements too: characters, atmosphere, emotions. In contrast, in Quevedo and also in Góngora, verbal structure is all there is. In my conversations with men of letters from other countries, I have found that they don't know Quevedo—with the exception, of course, of those who are Hispanists. Sometimes, they know there was a famous person by that name, and that is all.

I think it is impossible to translate him into foreign languages. The same holds true for Joyce—a virtually untranslatable author who nevertheless is famous the world over. I have always thought that perhaps Joyce can only be translated into German, however, he is known in almost every language—poorly translated, no doubt. I tremble when I hear one of my works has been translated. Who knows what meaning and what strange sonority my words will take on when translated into Japanese, Arabic or any other language?

22

Xul Solar

Once he asked me, rather naively, why
I didn't write in "creol." I told him that
the language was his invention and
that I had no right to write in "creol."
Then he said to me, "No, if it were
only my invention it wouldn't be worth
anything. Inventions must be collective.
If you find any book in 'creol' please
bring it to me, even if it's only a
cookbook, for it would be very strange
if I were the only one to discover that
language."

ALIFANO: Borges, you were one of the people who saw Xul Solar most
frequently. You were one of his closest friends. Can we talk about him?
What kind of a person was Xul?

BORGES: I have the happiest memories of Xul. But let's begin our talk, if
you will, with an assertion. I believe that Argentina, in the brief course of
its history, has produced three geniuses: the first, without a doubt, was
Domingo Faustino Sarmiento; and then, despite his gloominess, the poet
Almafuerte; and in the present century, the painter Alejandro Xul Solar,
whom I had the honor to befriend. Whenever I think of Xul, I feel the need
to compare him to William Blake; and a study could be done, I think,
about "the differences and affinities" between them, as Alfonso Reyes
once noted.

ALIFANO: Xul Solar was a great admirer of Blake, and the similarities
you note seem justified.

BORGES: Yes. Xul felt that Blake was his brother. Like Xul, Blake was a visionary and a poet. Moreover, Blake was a similar type of artist. Xul was a man with a universal curiosity. He was interested above all in languages. He invented two languages. One of them was the *"Pan Lengua"* (The Pan Language), which matched the *"Pan Juego"* (The Pan Game) and was based on astrology. The Pan Game is similar to chess but it is much more complicated than chess. It is played astrologically, with twelve squares on each side; that is, it has one hundred and forty-four squares, whereas chess has sixty-four. The movement of the pieces is, moreover, much more complicated than in chess; for if one piece takes another, it assumes the properties of the one it has taken. If the queen, for example, takes a knight, she could assume the movements of the knight. Now the game would run into problems: every time Xul explained it he would come up with innovations, and thus he kept on enriching it and invalidating many of its previous rules. I believe he never fully explained it because he was always thinking of further modifications.

ALIFANO: Was the Pan Game ever played?

BORGES: Yes, of course, despite the infinite modifications that Xul came up with! I remember once we were passing by a tea room at the corner of Santa Fé and Pueyrredón, and there were two disciples of Xul's playing his Pan Game. But it never became popular because of the changes Xul kept adding.

ALIFANO: Does he have any followers now?

BORGES: I really don't know what has happened to his followers. For a time he was surrounded by many young men who practiced his inventions, particularly in regard to painting—a field in which he was considered a master. And even today he is considered to be one. Xul had always had many followers.

ALIFANO: Was "creol" the other language invented by Xul Solar?

BORGES: Yes, that language was made up of Spanish enriched by neologisms and by monosyllabic English words that were used as adverbs. Xul always spoke in "creol." Once we were walking in an outlying barrio of Buenos Aires, in Chacarita, and he proposed that we go into a tavern called *"La Tapera"* to drink a glass of gin. The place was full of hoodlums, cart drivers, in short, all sorts of characters from the barrios. I was somewhat afraid of the place, but Xul was a regular customer, and I remember that he spoke with the other customers in "creol." All that seemed odd to me, but Xul conducted himself with complete ease and the others respected him. He was a man who had an air of authority about him. One of the customers we were with was shot to death by the police a few months later. That *guapo* had respected Xul and had been his friend. Xul Solar was exceptional. I never saw a man as courteous as he was and who at the same time commanded so much respect. He had an air of authority about him which even criminals recognized.

ALIFANO: You once said that Xul Solar had a very great talent for writing. Could he have been a great writer?

BORGES: I think so. I used to work for the Sunday supplement of the newspaper *Crítica*, and I would ask Xul to contribute articles. He never signed those articles because he was somewhat ashamed of them since they were written in regular Spanish and not in the languages he invented. Once I gave him a book about Tamerlaine to review, and a few hours later he returned with a masterful critique. It was an exposition on that character filled with his own highly original opinions and written with remarkable ease.

ALIFANO: What happened to the languages invented by Xul Solar? For example, did he induce anyone to speak "creol" or to write it?

BORGES: No. Regrettably, no. Once he asked me, rather naively, why I didn't write in "creol." I told him that the language was his invention and that I had no right to write in "creol." Then he said to me, "No, if it were only my invention it wouldn't be worth anything. Inventions must be collective. If you find any book in 'creol' please bring it to me, even if it's only a cookbook, for it would be very strange if I were the only one to discover that language."

ALIFANO: And in a day-to-day relationship what kind of person was Xul, Borges?

BORGES: Well, he was remarkably modest. To speak with him was a great experience for me. Xul always said interesting and intelligent things. Besides, I admired him greatly as a painter, and when I received my first paycheck from *Crítica*, the first thing I did was to run to his house to buy one of his paintings. I had received three hundred pesos and he was selling the painting I liked for a hundred pesos. Xul said he would give it to me for less since I was his friend. He charged me fifty pesos for the painting and gave me a much larger one as a present. He didn't handle his paintings as a business. The last thing he thought of was selling his work, which is very rare among painters.

ALIFANO: What is your opinion of his painting?

BORGES: It is the work of genius. Xul was not interested in the work of Picasso or Braque. He was closer to Paul Klee. But then I've been told that

Klee's work chronologically came after Xul's work. When Xul discovered the Swiss painter he was dazzled by his work. It was a true reaffirmation of the work he had been doing, perhaps for some time. I once asked Xul how he defined his own painting, and he told me that he considered himself a Realist painter, since the things he painted were what he saw in his visions.

ALIFANO: According to Lita, his wife, those visions he painted and to which he sometimes referred are found in his manuscripts.

BORGES: Yes, and those manuscripts are written in "creol" and in certain codes which make them difficult to decipher. *Sur*, Victoria Ocampo's magazine, could have published them, but Xul was seen as a willfully extravagant man. I remember that we were once invited to Victoria Ocampo's villa, and when Victoria came in, Xul got up and exclaimed: "The adverb has died!" He was referring to a person he had met on the street and who had bid him farewell by saying: " *Que te vaya lindo!*" (Hope all goes beautiful!) instead of "*lindamente*" (beautifully); he had used the adjective "beautiful" as an adverb. Then Victoria Ocampo, who didn't know a thing about grammar, interrupted him and said: "But Xul, what is all that stuff about the adverb? I don't know anything about grammar and I am not interested in it either." Of course, Victoria Ocampo was a self-taught woman who knew many things, but who ignored many others.

ALIFANO: Borges, what do you remember most fondly about your friend, Xul Solar?

BORGES: His capacity to make every conversation interesting. I was amazed by his manner of speaking. Xul was a man of genius and had extraordinary charm. He had the gift of *simpatía*. People who met him only once have a vivid and happy memory of that good, joyful and affectionate friend whose real name was Alejandro Oscar Xulz Solari. He abbreviated the name to Xul Solar, but he signed many of his paintings with the first two initials of his original name—AO. Which brings to mind the Tao, which means "the way" in Chinese. The *Tao Te Ching* is "The Book of the Way." And my friend was a pathway that we should keep on discovering.

23

Virgil

Virgil Today

Until the Romantic movement, which, in my opinion, began in Scotland around the middle of the eighteenth century and later spread throughout the world, Virgil was the poet par excellence. To me, in 1982, he is almost the archetypal poet. Voltaire justifiably wrote that if Homer had made Virgil, Virgil was his masterpiece. In the unfinished Aeneid *are gathered, as we know,* The Odyssey *and* The Iliad. *That is, the vast breadth of the epic and unforgettable brief lines. In the fourth* Georgics *we read: "In tenui labor." Beyond its context and its literal interpretation, those three words can sum up the delicate Virgil. Each tenuous line has been carved out. I remember now: "Agnosco veteri vestigia flammae" (I feel again a spark of that ancient flame). Dante, whose nostalgic love would dream up Virgil, translates it into that famous line: "Conosco i segni dell'antica flamma" (I recognize the tokens of the ancient flame).*

Virgil is Rome, and all of us Westerners of today are exiled Romans.

Jorge Luis Borges
Buenos Aires
September 1982

ALIFANO: Borges, throughout the ages there has been some controversy about that group of poems attributed to Virgil known collectively as *Appendix Virgiliana.* Croce has said that it's probable that some of his first poetic attempts are found in that collection, but that it is almost certain that he did not write all the poems. What is your opinion?

BORGES: Well, I concur with Croce, but I think that the issue is of no importance. In any case, it would be better if many of those poems were not by Virgil. In that collection there is a poem dedicated to the pizza—that rustic cake called *moretum* by Virgil—which I don't consider very good. Perhaps because I am not fond of pizza! But the issue, I contend, is not too important. Although, if some of those poems are not by Virgil, others, because of their excellence, deserve to be his. Now, I believe that the Virgil in whom we are all interested is found in the *Bucolics* or *Eclogues*, in the *Georgics* and in *The Aeneid*. In my opinion, the most interesting of the *Bucolics* is the fourth, where the poet proclaims the coming of a Golden Age, which will be announced by the birth of a divine child. For many years it was believed—perhaps it is true, who could possibly deny it—that in that remarkable poem Virgil had prophesied the birth of Christ.

ALIFANO: Now, Borges, leaving aside those details about the *Appendix*, which you deem unimportant, Virgil is the author of the *Georgics*—works of unquestionable and unsurpassed beauty, don't you think?

BORGES: Yes, certainly, they are unquestionably magnificent. Virgil composed them in Naples at the request of Maecenas, who intended to promote a movement of people to the countryside, a sort of agrarian reform supported by Augustus. Previously, Augustus had helped Virgil recover his lands, which Antony's supporters had taken away from him after the famous Battle of Philippi. The four books of the *Georgics*, curiously, deal with agriculture, with the raising of animals, with apiculture, and, I think, they also touch on the care of trees. All this is related in an admirable poetic tone. It has been said that it was one of the works Augustus admired most. In the last book Virgil tells us that if he were not near death, the moment of folding up the sails, he would sing of gardens.

ALIFANO: He fulfills that wish in *The Aeneid*. I believe he dedicated the last twelve years of his life to this book, didn't he?

BORGES: Yes, he did. In that epic poem Virgil sings of the fall of Troy, of the travels of Aeneas, and he passionately proclaims the evangelical mission of Rome as the leader of all human races.

ALIFANO: Many renowned readers of *The Aeneid* consider the sixth book the most beautiful and perfect of the twelve. Do you agree with that judgment?

BORGES: Yes, of course. One of the most beautiful memories I keep is that sixth book, where Virgil tells us about the voyage of the hero and of the Sybil of Avernus. There Aeneas finds the shadow of his father in the Elysian fields and receives encouragement from him and advice on how to face the terrible days that grow nearer. Following a poetic tradition of *The Odyssey*, he states that there are two divine gates of sleep through which dreams come to us: one made of horn, through which true dreams come, and one made of ivory, through which false or nonprophetic dreams come.

ALIFANO: What is the origin of that curious choice of imagery?

BORGES: I don't know, but I suppose that it all has to do with something that the poet felt very intensely. In his choice of images one could say that

Virgil perceives in an obscure way that dreams that foresee the future are less precious than nonprophetic or false dreams, which are the pure creations of the sleeping man.

ALIFANO: How strange that Virgil, shortly before his death, asked his friends to destroy his unfinished *Aeneid*!

BORGES: Yes, Kafka, in this century, asked his friend Max Brod to burn his work. Virgil did the same. Perhaps that is why *The Aeneid* ends, not unmysteriously, with the words "*Vitaque cum gemitu fugit indignata sub umbras*" (his life, resentful, fled to Shades below). Now I believe that deep down he did not want to have his work burned. If Virgil had wanted to destroy his work, he would have done it himself. He entrusted his friends to do it to free himself of a responsibility, not to compel them to carry out his order. His friends probably understood this and thus they did what was appropriate: they fulfilled the secret wish of the dead man. Fortunately, thanks to this intelligent disobedience, we have inherited that foremost work in the history of literature.

ALIFANO: Virgil has left his mark on all the poets of the world: Dante, Góngora, Quevedo, Tasso, Ariosto, Petrarch, who passionately studied Virgil and left a critical exposition of his texts. The list would be endless, wouldn't it, Borges?

BORGES: Yes, indeed. Dante, moreover, turns him into a symbol of the highest wisdom. For Dante, Virgil is his angel. The man from Northumbria despairs when his angel momentarily abandons him; Dante despairs when Virgil abandons him. "*Virgilio a cui per mia salute die'mi*" (Virgil, to whom I gave myself to be saved), Dante says.

ALIFANO: When did you discover Virgil's poetry?

BORGES: When I was a student in Geneva, in my Latin classes. Virgil dazzled me from the start. Since then I have never stopped reading him devotedly.

ALIFANO: What amazes you the most in Virgil's work, Borges?

BORGES: Well, many things amaze me—I would say almost everything. But I am constantly amazed by his manner of handling metrics, by his use of the hexameter, by his impressive descriptive power. Virgil always chooses the precise word, and everything he sings acquires a sacred eloquence. Bacon said once that Virgil is the most chaste and magnificent poet that the world has ever had. He is right: Virgil is the poetry of all times.

24

Oscar Wilde

His enemies may say that it is the only
thing he has; but to me to have charm
is fundamental. That accusation is like
saying this fellow is only a genius, or
that fellow is only an angel.

ALIFANO: Chesterton once said that the moment had come to speak of
Oscar Wilde and his work and to put aside certain sordid incidents of his
life. Do you care to speak about him, Borges?

BORGES: Well, it seems a good idea to me. I didn't know those words of
Chesterton's, but I remember that I once advised a friend of mine who was
writing a book on Wilde not to refer to those events which we all know, to
put them aside and to concentrate on his work, which is the central thing.
Wilde was a man with a tragic destiny, but I am sure that he didn't seek it
out; he always fought against becoming a tragic person. And I believe the
best proof of what I am saying is his work. Robert Louis Stevenson said
that there is a literary quality without which all other qualities would be
useless: that is the quality of charm. And, certainly, Oscar Wilde did not
lack charm. His enemies may say that it is the only thing he has; but to me
to have charm is fundamental. That accusation is like saying this fellow is
only a genius, or that fellow is only an angel. Now, in Wilde's case, when we
read him we feel that he still speaks to us, that he still amazes us. It is
strange to think that he died in 1900, because everything he said seems as
though it has just been said. That is, undoubtedly, the virtue of all good
literature: it always seems recent.

ALIFANO: Has Oscar Wilde's work been properly judged?

BORGES: Yes, but in a relative manner. I still maintain that it is a mistake
to admire Wilde's "The Ballad of Reading Gaol." That poem sounds
unconvincing to me. It deals with an English soldier condemned to be
hanged for having killed his mistress. If we analyze it somewhat, we find in
its first lines a fallacious notion: "He did not wear his scarlet coat," one of
the lines reads, "For blood and wine are red." The idea of an English

soldier of the 1890s drinking wine is absurd; undoubtedly, he would have drunk beer or hard liquor. Nor are the metaphors faithful to the character that Wilde presents. He speaks of the prisoners referring to the sky as a blue tent, and then he speaks of the clouds with their silver sails. To me, all that is foreign to the image of a soldier; they are mere decorative images and related more to Wilde himself and not in the least to the character. Kipling would never have made such a mistake; he would have become the soldier and would not have spoken of wine or silver sails or of a small blue tent. All those are decorative details and nothing else.

ALIFANO: What do you consider to be Wilde's most lasting work?

BORGES: His comedies. And, particularly, the comedy *The Importance of Being Earnest*.

ALIFANO: This comedy, according to the opinion of many critics, is very important to nineteenth-century English theater.

BORGES: Yes. Furthermore, I believe it is better than his other comedies simply because during the nineteenth century, inexplicably and curiously, theater in the land of Shakespeare, Marlowe and Ben Jonson had become a second-rate genre. And Oscar Wilde, who in his other plays had given way to sentimental plots and tried to save them or to disguise that quality with witticisms, suddenly produced *The Importance of Being Earnest*, a play free of sentimentality, although pleasantly frivolous. Now, of course, the sentimentality of Wilde is, to some extent, understandable. The theater in England at that time was sentimental. But I insist that Wilde to a very great extent helped to change it. Later came Bernard Shaw and Ibsen, and they opened a road of sincerity and freedom, changing it altogether. And now English theater is what it is thanks to them. However, I would say that *The Importance of Being Earnest* is, like champagne, a sort of fiesta; a very pleasant fiesta much like champagne, which is something more than a drink. And *The Importance of Being Earnest* is more than a comedy—it is a true sort of happiness.

ALIFANO: And his famous novel, *The Picture of Dorian Gray*, what place does that have in the work of Wilde?

BORGES: Perhaps mistakenly, the highest place. It is obvious that *The Picture of Dorian Gray* is an imitation of *Doctor Jekyll and Mister Hyde* by Robert Louis Stevenson. However, it is written in a very decorative and contrived manner. Stevenson's novel antedates *Dorian Gray* by almost ten years.

ALIFANO: There is a story by Poe which also deals with the theme of the double. I am referring to "William Wilson," that character who destroys himself in order to drown his heavy conscience. Do you remember it?

BORGES: Yes. But I had not thought of it. Perhaps that story was also influenced by Stevenson, since he came before it. The theme of the double is quite old; I have also been tempted by it many times. One of my stories, "The Other," deals with it. The concept of Oscar Wilde's character is, however, very curious: It is the concept of a man who keeps young while his portrait ages. In the last chapter Dorian Gray rips his portrait with a knife and dies. And then, there is that realistic detail which suits the story very well: The servants find the corpse of a man they cannot recognize; they find the destroyed portrait. And finally, they identify him by his clothes and rings.

ALIFANO: In Oscar Wilde's work, poetry has an important place. Shall we analyze it?

BORGES: Well, I believe that his best poem is "The Sphinx," which is a purely decorative poem. But it can become something else, since Wilde was a master of the decorative style. However, the merely decorative chapters that he interposes in *Dorian Gray* do not suit it, because they seem foreign to the order, to the bare structure of that novel. "The Sphinx," on the other hand, is made up of such elements and they are fitting. It is a musical and visual poem. Oscar Wilde has a spontaneous formal poetic expression and not a single experimental verse is found in all his work.

ALIFANO: Also, his vocabulary is curiously simple, isn't it?

BORGES: True. And it is so much so that if to study German it is convenient to begin with Heine's first poems, similarly, to study English I always recommend that the student should begin by reading Oscar Wilde. His vocabulary is made up mainly of words derived from Latin, which are difficult for English speakers but easy to us. So that I would advise someone who wants to learn English and who wants to have a pleasant time at it, to begin by reading Wilde's work.

ALIFANO: But let's go on talking about Oscar Wilde's poetry.

BORGES: Another of his important poems is "The Harlot's House." In it he describes the following scene: "Sometimes a clockwork puppet pressed/ A phantom lover to her breast,/ Sometimes they seemed to try to sing." Like almost all his other poems, that poem is decorative. Now, if we compare Oscar Wilde with poets such as Keats, Eliot, Tennyson and Rossetti, he was certainly a lesser poet, but the greatness of Wilde is found in his other works.

ALIFANO: What has happened to his work in England? How has he fared with time?

BORGES: Well, he is almost a forgotten poet there. Wilde is famous, however, in other parts of the world. Something similar has happened in the United States concerning Edgar Allan Poe, who, as a poet, was revived by Baudelaire and Mallarmé. In the United States Poe is judged by his poetry and not by his stories, which are of greater value. That poem by Poe, "The Raven," which is so famous, well, it is really a stuffed crow. Most probably Poe did not set out to write a great poem. What he set out to do was to write a poem that would make him famous, and he achieved that. As to Wilde, his esthetics are found in his dramatic dialogues, which are truly admirable.

ALIFANO: Was Oscar Wilde a man of genius?

BORGES: Well, I don't know if he was truly a man of genius, but there is no doubt that he was a man with an immense talent. Oscar Wilde once told André Gide that he had placed his genius in his life and his talent in his work. I suspect that Oscar Wilde was, moreover, an innocent being. I have read and reread the biography of Wilde written by Hesketh Pearson, which seems to me to be the best. And Pearson contends that Wilde was a reckless man. I believe that he was a mischievous spirit who was fond of playfulness. And he would have carried out that playfulness with the same intelligence within any literary movement—Cubism, Futurism, Impressionism, etc.—and always with a broad smile, which is what makes him different from other poets better than he, who perhaps influenced him, poets such as Mallarmé.

ALIFANO: Wilde once said that he conceived art as a game.

BORGES: Yes, and he delighted in amazing people with his metaphors. He was what Pliny defined as "*Monstrorum artifex*," which can be translated as "a maker of monsters." Wilde's work is full of artifices, which, in his case, could be used as an argument for his greatness as a writer.

ALIFANO: Oscar Wilde was a highly cultured man, isn't that so?

BORGES: Undoubtedly. He was a man who read a great deal. He knew Greek and Latin; he had studied the classics in their original languages. He spoke French as correctly as he spoke English. But he had the elegance to hide that knowledge; he possessed that curious ambition of appearing frivolous, banal. And yet he was not so. In his work one unexpectedly comes upon very profound thoughts, said in passing, which appear superficial but which, in fact, are not so. Take, for example, this very odd idea which I found in one of his works, that a man in every moment of his life is everything that he has been and everything that he will be. It is a very strange idea, but it is said as though in passing. Heraclitus had said: "A man's character is his destiny," which means the same, but which is said in a less beautiful manner. Oscar Wilde was a great writer, a cultured man with an immense talent who has left us a charming image: the image of a dandy who had to bear a tragic destiny, perhaps unaware of it, but which does not tarnish in the least the charm he has given us.

JORGE LUIS BORGES
A SELECTION OF POEMS

All poems translated by Willis Barnstone
except "1982," translated by Jorge Luis Borges,
and "Possession of Yesterday," translated by Nicomedes Suárez Araúz

From *EL OTRO, EL MISMO* (The Other, The Same), 1964

THE OTHER TIGER

I think of a tiger. Half-light exalts
The vast busy Library
And seems to set the bookshelves back;
Strong, innocent, bloodstained, fresh,
It wanders through its jungle and its morning
And prints its tracks on the muddy
Banks of a river whose name it doesn't know
(In its world there are no names or past
Or future, only a certain now)
And slips through barbaric distances,
Sniffing smells in the braided labyrinth
Out of the smell of dawn
And the delicious smell of deer;
Among the stripes of the bamboo tree
I decipher the tiger's stripes and feel
Its bony frame under the splendid quivering hide.
The curving seas and deserts of the planet
Futilely intervene;
From this house in a remote port
In South America I track you and dream you,
O tiger of the Ganges's banks.

As evening fills my soul I think
The tiger addressed in my poem
Is a tiger of symbols and shadows,
A string of literary tropes
And scraps from the encyclopedia
And not the fatal tiger, the deadly jewel
That under the sun or changing moon
Goes on in Sumatra or Bengal fulfilling
Its rounds of love, indolence and death.

To the tiger of symbols I oppose
The real one, with hot blood,
Decimating a herd of buffalos,
And today, August 3rd, 1959,
A deliberate shadow spreads over the grass
Yet in the act of naming it
And conjecturing its word, it becomes
A fiction, art, and not a living beast
Among beasts roaming the earth.
We will seek a third tiger. Like
The others it will be a shape
From my dream, a system of human words,
And not the vertebrate tiger
Which beyond mythologies
Paces the earth. I know all this,
Yet something drives me to this vague,
Insane and ancient adventure, and I go on,
Searching through the hours of the afternoon
For the other tiger, not in the poem.

POEM WRITTEN IN A COPY OF BEOWULF

At times I ask myself what are the reasons,
During my wandering night, that now impel
Me to begin (expecting no miracle
Of perfection) to study the tongue of the harsh Saxons.
Exhausted by the years my memory
Allows the futilely repeated words
To slip away, the way my life first girds
And then ungirds its tired history.
I tell myself it must be that the soul,
In a sufficient and a secret way,
Knows it is immortal, that its vast, grave
Circle takes in and can accomplish all.
Beyond this longing and beyond this verse,
Waiting for me, inexhaustible: the universe.

IN PRAISE OF SHADOW

Translated by Anthony and Willis Barnstone

Old age (this is the name that others give it)
may be the time of our happiness.
The animal is dead or nearly dead.
Man and his soul remain.
I live among vague and luminous forms
that are not yet darkness.
Buenos Aires,
which once was torn into far suburbs
facing the endless plain,
is now the cemetery of the Recoleta, the Retiro
    square,
the dingy streets of the Eleventh district,
and the precarious old houses
that we still call the South.
Always there were too many things in my life;
Demokritos of Abdera tore out his eyes to think;
time has been my Demokritos.
This penumbra is slow and brings no pain;
it flows down a gentle slope
and resembles eternity.
My friends have no faces,
women are what they were so many years ago,
one street corner might be another,
there are no letters on the pages of books.
All this ought to unnerve me,
but it is a sweetness, a return.
From the generations of texts on the earth
I have read only a few,

135

the ones I keep reading in memory,
reading and distorting.
From the South, the East, the West, the North,
roads converge that have led me
to my secret center.
Those roads were echoes and footsteps,
women, men, agonies, resurrections,
days and nights,
half-dreams and dreams,
every obscure instant of yesterday
and of the world's yesterdays,
the firm sword of the Dane and the moon
    of the Persian,
the deeds of the dead,
shared love, words,
Emerson and snow and so many things.
Now I can forget them. I reach my center,
my algebra and my key,
my mirror,
Soon I will know who I am.

THE UNENDING ROSE

to Susana Bombal

Five hundred years after the Hegira
Persia, from its minarets,
Watched the invasion of desert lances
And Attar of Nishapur looked at a rose
And spoke to it with tacit words
(Like one who thinks, not one who prays):
"Your vague sphere is in my hand. Time
Stoops us both and we are unaware
Of a lost garden this afternoon.
Your slight weight is moist in the wind.
The relentless high tide of your fragrance
Rises to my old declining face
But I know you are farther than the child
Who glimpsed you in the layer of a dream
Or here one morning in the garden.
The sun's whiteness may be yours
Or the moon's gold or the vermillion
Firmness of the sword in victory.
I am blind and know nothing, but I foresee
There are more roads. Each thing
Is infinite things. You are music,
Firmaments, palaces, rivers, angels,
An intimate, limitless, profound rose,
Which the Lord will show my dead eyes."

THAT NOTHING IS KNOWN

The moon can't know it is serene and clear,
Nor can it even know it is the moon;
Nor sand that it is sand. No thing may soon
Or ever know it has a strange form here.
The pieces made of ivory are as far
From abstract chess as is the hand, the key,
That guides them. Perhaps the human destiny
Of brief joy and lingering despair
Is the instrument of the Other. We can't know.
Giving it the name of god does no good.
And fear, doubt, and the midday prayer we could
Not finish—all that is futile. What bow
Could have relesed the arrow that I am?
What peak can be the target of that hand?

A BLIND MAN

I do not know what face looks back at me
When I look at the mirrored face, nor know
What aged man conspires in the glow
Of the glass, with tired silent fury.
Slow in shadow, with my hand I explore
My invisible features. A sparkling ray
Reaches me. A glimmer of your hair is gray
And some is even gold. I've lost no more
Than just the useless surfaces of things.
This consolation is of great import:
It is the comfort Milton had. I resort
To letters and to roses—my wonderings.
I think . . . if I could see my face I soon
Would know who I am on this rare afternoon.

I AM

I am the one who knows he is as vain
As the vain observer in the mirror of
Silence and glass, who looks upon the hov-
ering reflection or the body (the same)
Of his brother. I am, tacit friend,
The one who knows the only vengeance is
Oblivion. No other pardon. A god concedes
This curious key for hating fellow men.
I am the one who with a crystal ball
Of exploration still cannot decode
The singular and plural, sharp and bold
Labyrinth of time belonging to us all.
I am no one. In war I was no sword.
I am an echo, oblivion, a void.

THE BLIND MAN I

The varied world was plundered. Gone the sweep
Of faces (that are what they were before),
The nearby streets, today remote. And more,
The hollow blue that yesterday was deep.
Left in the books is only what remains
In memory—that form of forgetfulness
Which keeps the format but undoes the sense,
Reflecting mere titles. The street contains
Ambushing breaks and holes. And each step won
May be a fall. I am the very slow
Prisoner of a dreamlike time who has no
Way to mark his dawn or his declining sun.
It is night. No one is here. With my verse
I must work out my insipid universe.

THE BLIND MAN II

Since my birth, which was eighteen ninety-nine,
By a curved grape arbor and a deep well,
Meticulous time—brief in memory—designed
To rob me of the world's visible forms, which fell
Away. Days and nights filed the profiles of
The human letters and the faces that
I loved. My wasted eyes stared vainly at
Worthless libraries and lecterns. Above,
The blue and the vermillion are a cloud
And two useless words. The mirror I see
Is a gray thing. In the garden I breathe,
My friends, a desolate rose inside a shroud
Of darkness. Now, only yellow forms still glare
And I can only see to see nightmares.

ON HIS BLINDNESS

I am unworthy of the stars and bird
Furrowing the deep blue—now a secret:
Of those warped lines that are the alphabet
Which others use; of the marble grave blurred
And lost in shadow and whose lintel holds
Nothing for my now wasted eyes; of the
Invisible roses or the quietly
Imposing multitudes of reds and golds.
But I am not of A Thousand and One Nights
That open seas and daybreak in my dark;
Nor of Walt Whitman, the Adam who names, marks
The creatures under the moon nor of the white
Gifts of oblivion. I am lowly cast
For the love for which I hope and do not ask.

THE WHITE DEER

From what old border ballad out of green
England, from what Persian print or arcane
Regions of the days and nights that contain
Our past—came the white deer through the scene
I dreamed this morning? For a second. I saw
It cross the meadow and lose itself in gold
Of an illusory afternoon, a lithe creature mold-
ed from a bit of memory and the draw
Of oblivion—a deer on one side only then.
Numens who rule this strange world let me dream
Of you but not control you. Maybe in a seam
Of the deep future I will find you again,
White deer of a dream. I too am a dream in flight,
Lasting a few days more than the dream of field and white.

EPHIALTES*

At the bottom of dream are dreams. Each night
I want to lose myself in the dark waters
Washing me from day, yet an obscene wonder
Throbs under pure waters in a gray light
That gives us the hour of penultimate Void.
It may be a mirror with my strange face;
A prison growing in a labyrinth. The space
May be a garden. It is always destroyed:
A nightmare. An unwordly horror. Something
Unnamed reaches me from early days of myth
And mist; the hated image holds in the pit
Of the eye, and defames my wake and darkening.
Why, when my soul is alone and limbs repose,
Do I find—burgeoning in me—this maddening rose?

*Greek for the demon of nightmare

THE CONQUISTADOR

Carbajal and Cabrera were my names.
I've drained the full wineglass to the last dram.
Have died and I have lived many times. I am
The Archetype. The others, men. My claim:
For Spain and for the Cross I was the wan-
dering soldier. Through lands unexplored
Of an infidel continent I stirred up wars.
In fierce Brazil I carried the banner on.
Neither Christ nor my King nor red gold
Were the instigating spur of my bold-
ness which released a terror in the waves
Of pagans. My labor's reason was the beautiful
Sword and the tempestuous rage of battle.
All the rest does not matter. I was brave.

THE SUICIDE

In the night there will be no star,
There will be no night.
I will die and with me the sum
Of the intolerable universe.
I will erase the pyramids, the medals,
The continents and the faces.
I will erase the accumulation of the past.
I will make dust of history, dust of dust.
I am looking at the last sunset.
I hear the last bird.
I will nothingness to no one.

MY BOOKS

My books (which do not know I exist)
Are as much a part of me as this face
With gray temples and gray eyes
I look for hopelessly in the glass
And that I run my hollow hand over.
Not without a logical bitterness
I think the essential words
Expressing me are in those leaves
That do not know who I am, not in those I've written.
Better that way. The voices of the dead
Will tell me forever.

THE PANTHER

Behind the massive iron bars the panther
Will track its boring road incessantly,
Which is (unknown to it) its destiny
As a fated black jewel and prisoner.
There are a thousand panthers padding back
And forth, but the fatal panther in its cave
Is one and eternal on the straight track
Eternal Achilles plotted when he gave
Himself into the dream the Greek had dreamed.
It doesn't know of mountains and rich fields
With deer whose bellies quiver and would yield
Pleasure to its blind appetite. All seemed
A waste—the world's diversity. The day
Each one lives already has a fixed way.

BROWNING RESOLVES TO BE A POET

In these red labyrinths of London
I discover I have chosen
the most curious of human professions
unless, in their way, they all are.
Like the alchemists
who looked for the philosopher's stone
in slippery mercury,
I will make common words—
the gambler's marked cards, everyday coins—
release the magic they had
when Thor was the numen and uproar,
thunder and prayer.
In today's dialect
I will, in turn, say the eternal things;
I will try not to be unworthy
of Byron's grand echo.
The dust I am will be invulnerable.
If a woman shares my love
my verse will graze the tenth sphere of the concentric
    heavens;
if a woman disdains my love
I will make my sadness into music,
a deep river that goes on resounding in time.
I will live to forget myself.
I will be the face I glimpse and forget,
I will be Judas accepting
the holy mission to be a traitor.
I will be the mercenary soldier dying
without fear and faith,
I will be Polycrates who sees the horror
of the ring returned by fate,
I will be the friend who hates me.
The Persian will give me a nightingale and Rome the sword.
Masks, agonies, resurrections
will unweave and weave my luck
and sometimes I will be Robert Browning.

BRUNANBURH, 937 A.D.

Nobody at your side.
Last night I killed a man in the battle.
He was courageous and tall, from the bright stock of Anlaf.
The sword entered his chest, a little to the left.
He rolled on the ground and was a thing.
A thing for crows.
You will wait for him in vain, woman I haven't seen.
The ships that fled over the yellow water
Will not return him.
At the hour of dawn
Your hand will search for him out of dream.
Your bed is cold
Last night I killed a man in Brunanburh.

DREAM

When the clocks at midnight prodigally
Strike a generous time,
I will go farther than the oarsmen of Ulysses
To the region of dream, inaccessible
To human memory.
In this submerged region I salvage remains
That I cannot understand:
Herbs of a simple botany,
A somewhat distinct race of animals,
Dialogues with the dead,
Faces that are really masks,
Words in very ancient tongues,
And at times an incomparable horror
That day can bring us to.
I will be everyone or no one. I will be the other
Who without knowing it I am, who has seen
That other dream, my vigil. He judges it,
Resigned and smiling.

THE NIGHTINGALE

In what secret night out of England
Or from the constant incalculable Rhine,
Lost among the nights of my nights,
Could your voice charged with mythologies
Have reached my unknowing ear,
Nightingale of Virgil or the Persians?
Perhaps I never heard you, but your life
And mine are joined inseparably.
Your symbol was a wandering spirit
In a book of enigmas. The Sea
Nicknamed you siren of the forests
And you sing in Juliet's evening
And on the intricate Latin page
And from the pine groves of the other
Nightingale of Judea and Germany,
Heine joking, on fire, sad.
Keats heard you for everyone, forever.
Among the bright names the peoples
Of the earth have given you,
Not one is unworthy of your music,
Nightingale of the Darkness. The Moslem
Dreamed you in a rage of ecstacy,
His chest pierced by the thorn
Of the rose sun that reddens
With your deepest blood. Assiduously
In the evening I scheme this exercise,
Nightingale of the sand and of the seas.
In memory, in exaltation, in fable,
You burn with love and die melodiously.

HERACLITUS

Heraclitus is walking through the afternoon
Of Ephesos. With no intervention
Of his will the afternoon has left him
On the border of a soundless river
Whose destiny and name he does not know.
There is a stone Janus and some poplars.
He sees himself in the shifting mirror
And discovers and polishes the sentence
Which generations of mankind
Will not let slip away. His voice declares:
No one steps two times in the waters
Of the same river. He stops. He feels,
With the astonishment of a sacred horror,
That he too is a river and a flight.
He wants to recapture that morning
And its night and the night before. He cannot.
He repeats the sentence. He sees it printed
In future bright characters
On one of Burnet's pages.
Now Heraclitus does not know Greek. Janus,
God of the Gates, is a Latin god.
Heralictus has no yesterday or now.
He is a mere artifice that a gray man
Dreamed on the shores of the Red Cedar River,
A man who is weaving pentameters
So as not to brood so much on Buenos Aires
And on the loved faces. One face is gone.

A KEY IN EAST LANSING

I am a key whose steel has been filed out.
My uneven edge was not cut aimlessly.
I sleep my vague sleep in a closet I don't see
In which I am a captive held throughout
By my keychain. A lock waits for me within,
Only one. The door is made of forged steel
And tight glass. Inside, ready to reveal
Itself, is the hidden true house. Deep in
The scanty twilight, the uninhabited
Mirrors glare into the nights and days
And glare upon the photographs of the dead
And the tenuous past of photographs. In this maze,
One day I will push up against the rock—
Hard door, and slip inside to turn the lock.

East Lansing, Michigan
1976

REMORSE

I have committed the worst sin of all
That a man can commit. I have not been
Happy. Let the glaciers of oblivion
Drag me and mercilessly let me fall.
My parents bred and bore me for a higher
Faith in the human game of nights and days;
For earth, for air, for water, and for fire.
I let them down. I wasn't happy. My ways
Have not fulfilled their youthful hope. I gave
My mind to the symmetric stubbornness
Of art, and all its webs of pettiness.
They willed me bravery. I wasn't brave.
It never leaves my side, since I began:
This shadow of having been a brooding man.

NIGHTMARE

I am dreaming of an ancient king. His crown
Is iron and his gaze is dead. There are
No faces like that now. His rigid sword
Will watch over him, loyal like his hound.
I do not know if he is from Norway
Or Northumberland. But from the north, I know.
His thick red beard capes his chest. He doesn't throw
A glance at me, not a blind glance my way.
From what blackened mirror or from what ship
On seas that were his gambling wilderness
Could this gray and grave man venture a trip
Toward me, imposing his past and bitterness?
I know he dreams and judges me, is drawn
Erect. Day breaks up night. He has not gone.

EIN TRAUM

The three of them knew it.
She was Kafka's companion.
Kafka had dreamed about her.
The three of them knew it.
He was Kafka's friend.
Kafka had dreamed about him.
The woman told the friend:
Tonight I want you to love me.
The three of them knew it.
The man answered: If we sin,
Kafka will quit dreaming about us.
One found out.
There was nobody left on the earth.
Kafka said to himself:
Now that they are gone, I am alone.
I will stop dreaming about myself.
Nobody found out.

JOHANNES BRAHMS

I who am an intruder in those gardens—
which you have lavished on the plural memory
of the future—wished to sing of that glory
immersed in blue and raised by your violins
But I've given up. To honor you
that misery (which people like to save
by shrilly invoking art) will never do.
To honor you one must be bright and brave.
I am a coward, a sad man, and know
that nothing will redeem my resolution
to sing of the magnificent elation—
fire and crystal—of your loving soul.
My servitude is the impure word, impure
conjunction of a concept and a sound.
Not a symbol, not a mirror, not a moan,
yours is the river that flows and will endure.

G. L. BÜRGER

I can never quite understand
Why I am so bothered by the thing
That happened to Bürger
(his dates are in the encyclopedia),
there, in one of the cities on the plain,
next to the river which has only one bank,
where the palm tree grows, not the pine.
Like all other men,
he told and heard lies,
betrayed and was betrayed,
often agonized over love,
and after sleepless night
saw the gray winter panes of dawn,
but he merited the great voice of Shakespeare
(in which others are heard)
and the voice of Angelus Silesius of Breslau,
and with affected carelessness he polished a line
the way others did in his day.
He knew the present to be nothing
but a fleeting particle of the past
and that we are made of oblivion,
of wisdom useless as Spinoza's corrollaries
or the wonders of fear.
In the city by the still river,
about two thousand years after a god's death
(the story I refer to is ancient),
Bürger is alone and now,
precisely now, he is polishing a few lines.

THE CAUSES

The sunsets and the generations.
The days and none was the first.
The freshness of water in Adam's
Throat. Orderly Paradise.
The eye deciphering the darkness.
The love of wolves at dawn.
The word. The hexameter. The mirror.
The Tower of Babel and pride.
The moon which the Chaldeans gazed at.
The uncountable sands of the Ganges.
Chuang-Tzu and the butterfly that dreams him.
The golden apples on the islands.
The steps in the wandering labyrinth.
Penelope's infinite tapestry.
The circular time of the Stoics.
The coin in the mouth of the dead man.
The sword's weight on the scale.
Each drop of water in the water-clock.
The eagles, the memorable days, the legions.
Caesar on the morning of Pharsalis.
The shadow of crosses over the earth.
The chess and algebra of the Persians.
The footprints of long migration.
The sword's conquest of kingdoms.
The relentless compass. The open sea.
The clock echoing in the memory.
The king executed by the axe.
The incalculable dust that was armies.
The voice of the nightingale in Denmark.
The calligrapher's meticulous line.
The suicide's face in the mirror.
The gambler's card. Greedy gold.
The forms of a cloud in the desert.
Every arabesque in the kaleidoscope.
Each regret and each tear.
All those things were made perfectly clear.
So our hands could meet.

ENDYMION ON LATMOS

I was sleeping on the summit and my body
Was beautiful, now worn out by years.
High in the Hellenic night, the centaur
Slowed his fourfold race
To spy into my dream. I liked
To sleep in order to dream and for the other
Lustrous dream eluding memory
That purifies us from the burden
Of being what we are on earth.
Diana, goddess who is also the moon,
Saw me sleeping on the mountain
And slowly came down into my arms
Gold and love in the flaming night.
I held her mortal eyelids,
I wanted to see her lovely face
Which my lips of dust profaned.
I tasted the moon's perfume
And her unending voice called my name.
O pure faces seeking each other,
O rivers of love and of night,
O human kiss and the bow's tension.
How long has my wandering lasted?
There are things unmeasured by grapes
Or flower or slender snow.
People run from me, are threatened
By the man loved by the moon.
Years have gone by. One worry
Horrifies my vigil. I wonder
If that uproar of gold in the mountain
Was true or merely a dream.
Why fool myself that a memory
Of yesterday and a dream are the same?
My loneliness drifts along the ordinary
Roads of the earth, but in the ancient night
Of the Numens, I always seek
The indifferent moon, daughter of Zeus.

THE MOON

for María Kodama

There is such loneliness in that gold.
The moon of the nights is not the moon
Which the first Adam saw. The long centuries
Of human vigil have filled her
With ancient lament. Look at her. She is your mirror.

A SATURDAY

A blind man in an empty house
Wears out certain limited routes
And touches the lenghtening walls
And the glass of interior doors
And the rough spines of books
Denied to his love and the darkened
Silverware passed down from his family
And water faucets and moldings
And some spare coins and the key.
He's alone and no one's in the mirror,
Coming and going. His hand grazes
The bookshelf edge. Unintentionally,
He's stretched out in the lonely bed
And feels that the acts he performs
Interminably in the dusk
Obey a game he doesn't understand,
Which an indecipherable god directs.
Aloud and in cadence he repeats
Fragments of the classics and tries out
Variations of verbs and epithets,
And good or bad he writes this poem.

MUSIC BOX

Music of Japan. Drops of slow honey
Or of invisible gold are dispersed
In a miserly way from the water clock,
And repeat in time a weaving that is
Eternal, fragile, mysterious and clear.
I fear that each one may be the last.
It's a past coming back. From what temple,
From what light garden in the mountain,
From what vigil before an unknown sea,
From what shyness of melancholy,
From what lost and ransomed afternoon
Does its remote future come to me?
I cannot know. No matter. I am
In that music. I want to be. I bleed.

1982

A heap of dust has gathered in the depths of the shelf, behind the
row of books.
My eyes do not see it. It is a cobweb to my touch.
It is but a point of that other web we call the history of the world
or the cosmic process.
It is but a point of the web that encircles stars, deathbeds, migrations,
thorns, agonies, vigils, pyramids, glow worms, Carthage and
Shakespeare.
A point of the web are also this page, that may not be a poem, and
the dream you had this morning, at dawn, and that you have altogether
forgotten.
Has the web a meaning? Schopenhauer believed it to be as senseless
as the faces or lions we make out in the shifting shapes of a cloud.
Has the web a meaning? The meaning cannot be ethical, since ethics
is an illusion of men, not of the unfathomable gods.
Perhaps the heap of dust may be no less useful to the aims of the
web than the ships loaded with an empire or the scent of a rose.

POSSESSION OF YESTERDAY

I know the things I've lost are so many that I could not begin to count them
and that those losses
now, are all I have.
I know that I've lost the yellow and the black and I think
of those unreachable colors
as those that are not blind can not.
My father is dead, and always stands besides me.
When I try to scan Swinburne's verses, I am told, I speak with my father's voice.
Only those who have died are ours, only what we have lost is ours.
Ilium vanished, yet Ilium lives in Homer's verses.
Israel was Israel when it became an ancient nostalgia.
Every poem, in time, becomes an elegy.
The women who have left us are ours, free as we now are from misgivings,
from anguish, from the disquiet and dread of hope.
There are no paradises other than lost paradises.